Explosive Ergogenics for Athletes:
Using the Science of Nutrigenomics to Maximize Performance

Rick Brunner

Published by:
Ultimate Athlete Concepts
Michigan, USA
2013

ISBN 978-0-9896198-3-7

Explosive Ergogenics for Athletes:
Using the Science of Nutrigenomics to Maximize Performance

Table of Contents

Nutrigenomic Ergogenics 1

Why Nutrition Ergogenics Specifically for Explosive Athletes? 3

The Mystique behind Soviet Sport Nutrition 6

THE TRAINING-ERGOGENIC CONNECTION 22

Contraction-Induced Signal Transduction Pathways in Exercised Muscle 26

AMP-Activated Protein Kinase Signaling (AMPK) 27

Skeletal Muscle Protein Synthesis via Contractions and Nutrient Stimuli 31

Nutrient-Gene Interactions (Nutrigenomic) for Muscle Building and Fat Burning 32

Nutrigenomic Anabolic Networks of Athlete Adaptation:

    Maximizing Muscle Mass, Strength, and Explosiveness 34

Building Muscle Proteins: The Parts and the Assembly 36

PROTEIN 36

The Amazing Amino Acid L-Leucine 42

CREATINE MONOHYDRATE 51

TRI-METHYL GLYCINE (TMG, GLYCINE BETAINE) 58

OMEGA-3 FATTY ACIDS 63

PHOSPHATIDIC ACID 70

MINERAL OROTATES 73

TAURINE 79

PLANT BASED ECDYSTERONES 81

ADDITIONAL NUTRITIONAL ANABOLIC ERGOGENICS 89

ENERGETIC ERGOGENICS 98

The Pre-Workout Supplement Boondoggle 100

Table of Contents (continued)

CAFFEINE	102
MINERAL SUCCINATES	106
BETA-ALANINE (β-alanine)	108
D-RIBOSE	113
ATP BOOSTERS	117
LIPOLYTIC - THE BURNING OF FATS	118
Fighting Excess Body Fat With Power, Not Endurance	120
AMPK/PGC-1α Activators	121
ADAPTOGENIC	132
NEUROLOGIC ERGOGENIC NUTRIENTS	147
The Neuromuscular Junction and Explosiveness	150
Reducing Acetylcholinesterase for Timely Powerful Muscle Contractions	152
CONCUSSION	160
Ricks Brain Trauma Prevention and Restorative Cocktail	162
THOUGHTS ABOUT YOUR BASE DIET	166
AVOID SPECIFIC SPORT NUTRITION INGREDIENTS OR PAY THE PRICE	169
AMPK Activating Nutrients and Explosive Training	174
SHOPPING FOR NUTRITIONAL ERGOGENICS	174
PUTTING ALL THIS NEW INFORMATION TO PRACTICAL USE	177
Rx PLANS	178

The nutrition and training information/programming contained in this book are based upon modern scientific research and the personal and professional experiences of the author. This information is not intended to replace or substitute for counsel from your personal physician, trainer, and/or coach. The nutritionals outlined in this book are focused on athletic performance and are not intended to treat, prevent, or cure any disease. The publisher and author are not responsible for any adverse effects or consequences resulting from the use of any nutritionals or programs discussed in this book.

Nutrigenomic Ergogenics

Ergogenics: Any pharmacological, nutritional, mechanical, or psychological aid that can improve athletic performance. This books focus is on the science of nutrigenomic ergogenics- how key dietary nutrients help turn on performance genes in explosive athletes. It covers what competitive athletes should consume through their diet and nutritional supplements that will help them become a better athlete. It also covers what athletes should not consume- nutrients which interfere with the adaptive response to explosive training that hinders athletic performance.

Ultimately the goal of nutrigenomic ergogenics is to amplify an explosive athlete's adaptation to intense sport-specific training. This will improve the neuromuscular traits essential for winning such as faster reaction, more starting power, maximal speed, increased striking force, and power-endurance to perform at a high level over-and-over.

When you're finished reading this book you'll have learned things that few in the world up until now know. You will have the "know-power" to design and implement a better training plan to build explosive traits because you will know how nutrients work to activate anabolic, energetic, adaptogenic, and neurologic gene pathways.

"We all have dreams. But in order to make dreams come into reality, it takes an awful lot of determination, dedication, self-discipline, and effort."
~ Jesse Owens

Why This Book?

I haven't written a full-blown book since I co-authored one titled "Soviet Training and Recovery Methods" with Dr. Ben Tabachnik back in 1990. This book is overdue.

There's a lot of misinformation about sport nutrition that conflicts with new well-designed scientific research, many real-world training applications, and even common sense. Sadly, we live in an uninformed world hijacked by big business and sound-bite sabotage, where undereducated and confused athletes, coaches, and parents haphazardly buy "sport" supplements based on brand perception that often lags reality by ten years or more. This false doctrine is perpetuated by sport nutrition companies that really know little about the science of sport nutrition, especially how it interacts with the training plan. The real key to success in sport is the merging of smart training with good nutrition.

Training leads the way by turning on certain gene pathways while ergogenic nutrition supplements amplify this pathway in anabolic and neurologic ways that build a more explosive athlete. Yet many sport nutrition companies never spend the time to really understand the training-ergogenic link. As such, they risk basing their formulas on antiquated science that doesn't follow the truths of modern-day sport nutrition science. Sometime this is just ignorance, while other times it is a deliberate denial of scientific truths just to make a buck. I would rather have a supplement I can trust rather than be fed some hype from a supplement company that says "trust me."

As an athlete, coach, parent of a young athlete, team trainer, or physician, you deserve the truth about ergogenic sport nutrition so you can rise up against the marketing hype and utilize the right nutrients in the right dose at the right time, without the noise of "dis-adaptive" nutrients that take away from the training result. The goal is to amplify the training effect with good nutrition ergogenics.

Over the past decade I've focused much of my attention toward anti-aging research, inflammation, and muscle loss in the elderly called sarcopenia. With an aging America it's important to understand why muscles become resistant to growth while, at the same time, it's easier for an aging person to grow fat cells. This aging research helped me to write this book, with the focus on how to help middle school to elite and professional level athletes build explosiveness. If I can build muscle mass and strength in a 70 year old grandma, which I can with careful program design, I can show you how to build greater athletic explosiveness during your peak years of performance potential. Knowing the genetic pathways that can maximize anabolism (muscle growth) and neuromuscular response (explosiveness) and do this drug free is now possible. I will show you how.

Knowledge is power. Explosive athletes and their coaches need a modern book on nutrition ergogenics because for too long recovery programs have been hijacked by uneducated messages focused on bodybuilding and bent on baffling athletes with "puffspeak" and pseudoscience, as well as scientific terms nobody but a PhD in exercise biochemistry can understand. There is a better way.

After reading this science based book I know you'll be empowered to introduce the right nutrients in the right amount and at the right time to synergize with your training- to efficiently and effectively switch on your explosive genes. I've written the book with an extensive science backdrop. I've written it just like I speak to athletes and coaches- in a way they can understand and apply for great results. There aren't too many ergogenic nutritionals that work for every athlete all the time. We're all just too different. Our genes are different and our training plans are different. I'll show you how to leverage your individuality to get the most from your training via ergogenic nutrition.

Why Nutrition Ergogenics Specifically for Explosive Athletes?

As an athlete, coach, and scientist for over 30 years, I've witnessed the evolution of performance nutrition firsthand. During the 1970's and early 1980's there were few choices for athletes. As a football lineman and shot putter in high school, and a hammer thrower in college, I trained clean. No anabolic steroids, but also no supplements either. Just good food. I did well in sports, starting on my high school varsity football team, and as league and regional champion in the shot put. In college I was an All-American in the hammer throw. What I know now about nutrition could have helped me to become a better athlete, a much better athlete.

Today nutrition is a different game. The variety of dietary supplements including drinks, powders, gels, pills, and bars is great. The sport nutrition industry today is a multi-billion dollar business- BIG BUSINESS. Most sport supplements sold today fall into two main categories- bodybuilding nutrition and endurance nutrition. And most of these are for the masses, like all the rehydration drinks, nutrition bars, and all-in-one powders sold by mass retailers and grocery stores. They are hardly specialized enough, or ergogenic enough, to do an explosive athlete much good.

Real Science. Real Results. No Fluff.

Fortunately the science of performance nutrition has exploded in just the past 10 years. Thanks a bunch to the internet, researchers are now able to share information with others worldwide and to collaborate on and publish this research much faster.

When I started my research career in the late 1980's I had to communicate with scientists by letter, telex, or fax. Calling a researcher in the Soviet Union back then was next to impossible and very nerve wracking. I can still recall the strange dial tone on the other end in Moscow. Finding useful papers was a tough haul too as I had to plough through volumes of reference books, locate a "few" journals in the stacks, and burn through rolls of quarters to copy any useful research I was lucky to locate at UC Davis (Carlson Medical), Stanford (Lane Medical), or UC Berkeley (Koshland BioSci) libraries.

Today, with the click of a mouse, I can not only access thousands of useful peer-reviewed journal articles, I can also email the principal author and ask questions about their research. Communication via email and Skype® is sizably improved and this helps advance ergogenic nutrition breakthroughs. Yet these nutrition breakthroughs, contained in thousands of published scientific papers, still need to reach athletes and coaches in a way they can understand and put to good use. It's necessary to get good science out of journals and into real-world training.

Checking all the way back to 1960, 65% of the research published on sport nutrition, some 3,200 papers have been published in just the past ten years. Plus, many more studies today are conducted on competitive athletes, even elite athletes. This new research greatly advances what we know about how nutrients influence our genes and ultimately, our athletic performance. Much more is now known about how proteins and specific amino acids, plant based compounds, minerals, and fatty acids help to amplify the adaptive response to sport specific training- to help build a more explosive athlete.

And a sizable amount of research has also shown what athletes should not consume, what I call the dis-adaptive nutrients. If you want to measurably improve your performances then you need to know which nutrients will help amplify your training and the adaptive response that follows. You also need to know which nutrients can be adaptive landmines that will sabotage your ability to make gains. It all comes down to switching on or off certain genetic and metabolic pathways to benefit your intense training.

I've organized much of this book to efficiently target the essential anabolic, energetic, lipolytic, neurologic, and adaptogenic pathways. Before you plough into the guts of the book and learn which nutrients turn on and off these pathways I want you to get a good feel about where I'm coming from as a scientist. Whenever I read a really interesting scientific paper I almost always check what other works the scientist has written about. I want to know how they evolved in their research and what brought them to this new paper. Only after examining thousands of published papers can I really know what's true and what's unanswered. Only with a deep-dive into the science can I come to a logical conclusion as to what may work and what likely will not work when it comes to ergogenic nutrients in athletic performance. No marketing hype, just lots of robust science.

Many athletes and coaches, once they learn that my early sport nutrition education evolved from many trips to Russia in the late 1980's and early 90's, want to know more about what made the Soviet athletes so dominant in international sports. I'm happy to share my experiences as they have sizably helped shape my research and coaching.

After a look at the Soviet system of sport nutrition I'd like to personally address athletes, coaches, team physicians, and parents of young athletes individually as to how ergogenics can, with proper application within the training plan, boost performance and improve health.

"Gold medals aren't really made of gold. They're made of sweat, determination, and a hard-to-find alloy called guts."
~ *Dan Gable, 1972 Olympic Gold Medalist in Wrestling*

The Mystique Behind Soviet Sport Nutrition

In 1986 I made a career path change and became involved in a new start-up sport nutrition company called Champion Nutrition. Run out of a warehouse in Fairfield, California, the drivers behind Champion were Mike Zumpano as owner and supplement formulator (Mike Z also introduced Cytomax®), Mike Walls (Mike W later founded Sportpharma and Promax Bar) as general manager, Bob Fritz (Bob formulated Muscle Milk® for Cytosport) as sales manager, and Ed Byrd (Ed co-founded EAS with Anthony Almada and he founded MRI sport nutrition) as salesperson. This was one great bunch of creative budding talents, all working under one roof during the mid 1980's.

During Champion's start up there weren't a lot of companies selling sport supplements. Much of what was available were old-school protein powders, carbohydrates like Carboplex® (maltodextrin, glucose polymer) by Unipro (Mike Z and Bob came from Unipro), liver tablets, and some multivitamins. The choices were pretty slim. We're talking the era of Gatorade® in just lemon lime, fruit punch, and orange flavors in a wide mouth glass bottle. That was it. No energy drinks or vitamin waters.

Champion Nutrition introduced Metabolol® which was an all-in-one high carb and moderate protein powder drink mix with added vitamins and minerals. For its day it was a revolutionary formula. Up until then many of the ingredients had to be purchased separately. In addition to Metabolol® Champion Nutrition introduced a few other products, one being Muscle Nitro® which contained mineral succinates (succinic acid bound to Ca, Mg, and K) with added branched chain amino acids (BCAA). It was the succinates we were working with that caught my attention and sent me on a science-based path I have never left.

Mike Zumpano got his hands on some scientific abstracts (summaries) about the influence of mineral succinates in cell energetics and mitochondria activity. The research was authored by a Russian scientist by the name of Maria Kondrashova from Puschino, about 70 miles south of Moscow. Puschino is the home of a leading scientific research center of the Russian Academy of Sciences.

During the 80's I like many athletes and coaches in the west was hungry for any bit of information coming out of the USSR as to how their athletes trained. This was still before the fall of the Berlin wall and the breakup of the Soviet Union. The Soviet athletes dominated international sports, especially sports like Olympic weightlifting, sprints, jumps, and throws in track and field, wrestling, and many others. I wanted to know how they got so good. In 1986 I embarked on a journey that would take me to the highest levels of Soviet Sport. I wrote Dr. Kondrashova and we began a dialogue. I found Maria open to collaboration and I learned a bunch about succinates and other restorative/energetic compounds from her research. This gave me the confidence to pursue the works of other scientists and coaches from the USSR.

By 1988 I was hooked. I was so fascinated (still from afar) by what the Soviets were doing when it came to nutrition and performance enhancing supplements that I knew I had to learn much more. So I hooked up with a group from the National Strength and Conditioning Association (NSCA) and traveled with them to Bulgaria and Russia. Our group, led by Ken Kontor, the organizations executive director, was comprised of many strength and conditioning coaches from around the world and me as the lone professional with a focus on performance nutrition. I roomed with Darryl Eto (now Director of Strength and Conditioning for the NBA Houston Rockets) and relied on his knowledge of the training side of athletic performance which would prove really helpful later. Darryl no doubt has some stories of our travels; especially the time I got us lost on the Moscow subway and, fortunately, thanks to my ability to speak a little broken Russian, hailed a cabbie out in the boondocks who drove us the several miles back to the sport hotel where we were staying. What a relief!

Darryl was working for Don Chu at Athercare in Castro Valley, California at the time and so I got to know Don as well. Following in the footsteps of Dr. Michael Yessis who introduced plyometrics to American athletes, Don used these plyometrics methodics to educate and train many elite athletes including the Golden State Warriors.

The NSCA trip to Bulgaria was mainly to witness the unique training of the Bulgarian Olympic Weightlifting team and receive coaching advice from their head coach Ivan Abadjiev and coach Angel Spassov. I was fortunate to be able to peel off from some of the training lectures and spend some quality time with the team's physician, discussing dietary supplements for performance enhancement with him. It was during this meeting that I learned of several novel supplements that I had never been exposed to before. I was given some to bring home. They were bottles of pills and vials of liquids for injection. You could no way bring that stuff back to the USA today.

The next leg of our trip was to the Central Institute of Physical Education and Sport in Moscow, Russia for a week of coaching lectures. It was lucky for me that I was the only member of the group with expertise and interest in performance nutrition. I got invited to a nutrition roundtable with leading Russian nutrition scientists. The Russians were interested to know what we were doing in the USA regarding nutritional ergogenics as much as my interest in what they were researching and prescribing to athletes. I learned that they had a detailed method of programming certain supplements during various times of the training cycles. This was opposite of what we were doing in the USA which was to take supplements constantly, often in the wrong dose, used with the wrong training. While many of our supplements were focused on bodybuilding, the Soviet program had a more refined and targeted program directed toward performance enhancement in explosive athletes. I liked this focus.

A young Ivan Abadjiev, former Olympic weightlifter and head coach of the Bulgarian Weightlifting Federation. During his career Ivan produced 12 Olympic champions, 57 world champions and 64 European champions. He continues to coach today in Danville, California. Brunner Photo. Bulgarian Olympic Weighlifting Camp, Varna, Bulgaria, 1988.

I was able to make some excellent contacts during the visit to Moscow. One researcher I got to know professionally was Professor Yuri Verkoshansky, whom many of you have likely met or at least read his books. Yuri is recognized as the inventor of the shock method of training, or what is often called plyometrics. He was a pioneer in the research of explosive strength training for the Soviet sport program. Yuri's lifelong work enlightened me as to the training side of explosive performance and how one must marry the nutrition side with sound training methodics to create true synergy. In other words, a trait (maximal strength, strength-endurance, speed, reaction, etc.) is stimulated in training and then nutritionals- mainly in recovery, further amplify the adaptive (anabolic, energetic, neurologic, lipolytic, and/or adaptogenic) pathways for a superior result.

Professor Yuri Verkoshansky, former head of the Russian Central Institute of Physical Culture and Sport Scientific Research Laboratory in Moscow and Scientific Consultant to the National Olympic Committee of Italy in his later years. Brunner Photo. State Central Institute of Physical Culture, Moscow, Russia, 1988.

After the NSCA trip to Bulgaria and Russia I was energized to put what I learned into practice. I was also very focused on what else I could bring to the USA from behind the Iron Curtain. It was a rush for me to travel to the Soviet Union and learn new things that no one else in the west had ever been exposed to. My trip to Russia in 1988 was the first of many.

Making several scientific contacts proved beneficial as I was invited to attend an international symposium on sport science held at the Research Institute of Physical Culture in Leningrad (now Saint Petersburg). At this symposium I was able to connect with many leading scientists from around the world. Of special note were my interactions with Professor Eric Hultman from the famous Karolinska Institute in Stockholm, Sweden, Atko Viru from the University of Tartu in Estonia, and Nikolai Volkov from Moscow. These three researchers opened my eyes to even more performance enhancing supplements, not the least of which was a new supplement called creatine.

Sergey Popov, Rick Brunner and Yuri Verkoshansky. Post-Symposium celebration. State Central Institute of Physical Culture, Moscow, Russia, 1988.

On a trip to view the Hermitage Museum in Leningrad we were making small talk and I mentioned that I was developing a new amino acid based powder supplement (Aminofit) for elite athletes, and that I was interested in adding something to make it even more anabolic. Nikolai suggested I add "creatine" to the powder. Now this was in 1988 and the first papers published on creatine monohydrate didn't come out until the early 1990's. Russian sport scientists were already working with this material years prior.

I really didn't know creatine monohydrate would turn out to be so popular until later on when this single nutrient helped transform a company started by Anthony Almada and Ed Byrd called EAS®. The introduction in 1992 of Phosphagen which was pure creatine monohydrate was the platform supplement for EAS®, helping it become a multi-million dollar success story.

Aminofit, with its added creatine monohydrate was a very effective anabolic, but due to the di- and tri-peptide amino acids which were very bitter, the powder tasted, according to some athletes, and rightfully so, "like monkey ass." This taught me a valuable lesson: That athletes will not consume a supplement, even if it is the most anabolic one around, if it does not taste good. Formulation lesson learned.

Other professional influences in my study and application of performance enhancing nutritionals as ergogenics include interactions with Dr. Sergey Portugalov, Chief Nutrition Advisor to the Russian Olympic Team and Director of the Laboratory of Biologically Active Substances in Moscow, Dr. Israel Brekhman, considered the leading researcher on adaptogenic substances, and Dr. Michael Kalinski who directed the Ukranian sport biochemistry program. I have many good memories and learning's from these experts as well as many others over several years traveling to Russia.

Rick Brunner and Dr. Michael Kalinski, Chair of the Department of Sport Biochemistry and Vice President of the Kiev State Institute of Physical Culture. Brunner Photo, Kiev, Ukraine, 1990.

I don't want you to take away from this historical account of my early years with sport nutrition as the be-all end-all. In the 1980s and 90's the Soviets simply had a different focus on nutritional ergogenics which was a more sport specific focus as to their use with competitive athletes. They studied nutrients on competitive speed-strength athletes.

While it's common knowledge now that many athletes from the former East Bloc, including East Germany, used banned performance enhancing drugs (PED's) they also use a number of nutrients that are safe and legal to help them achieve sport dominance. Today there are great opportunities to advance the science of nutrition ergogenics as they relate to explosive athletes, thanks to a number of major breakthroughs, not the least of which is mapping the human genome and specific in vitro (cell culture) and in vivo (in animal or human) tests. This has lead scientists to fine-tune the use of specific nutrients to enhance adaptation to training, especially in well-trained and elite athletes.

Bulgarian Olympic weightlifter at the National training camp in Varna, Bulgaria. Brunner Photo.

A Message to Competitive Athletes, Coaches, Trainers, and Parents of Young Athletes

The ideal laboratory for studying how various ergogenic nutritionals influence the training result is the actual real-world conditioning programs of athletes, ranging from beginner to professional, and even masters age athletes.

Coaching over 2,500 athletes since 1988 has allowed me to collect a large amount of observational data as to how various nutrients perform under diverse training situations with young boys and girls, and older men and women athletes from a wide variety of sports. While I've rarely seen any gender variation I have noticed differences between age groups and levels of ability. Here's my take on supplements for children, teens, young adults, mature adults, and seniors who compete at the masters level.

Child Athletes and their Parents

Children, even if they are in well-structured training programs such as gymnastics, soccer, track, Little League baseball, or pee-wee football for example do not require ergogenic supplements in most cases. They do need to eat nutritious foods, especially organic plant based foods (i.e. greens, fruits, seeds and nuts, colored rice) and lean meats, preferably organic raised. They need to get enough quality calories to maintain good growth and adapt to training properly. They also need a good source of calcium and other minerals from dark leafy greens and low-fat dairy products for good bone growth. Calcium/magnesium supplements should be considered for athletes in sports like gymnastics where weight management is of concern as these athletes are known to have low bone density. Extra protein supplements can be added to the diet if necessary to support anabolism. Omega-3 oils such as high quality fish oil rich in EPA and DHA can be added to help develop the brain and nervous system.

Ideally, child athletes should participate in a variety of sports and movements (like jumping on a trampoline, climbing, tag, and dodge ball) that are fun and also develop a good sense of balance and spatial awareness. This is a critical window of opportunity that sets the foundation for physical, cognitive, and neuromuscular abilities vital for elite athlete traits later on. Plus, social skills and hard effort at times that include both successes and failures, winning and losing, provide valuable teaching moments that build character.

Today kids have a lot of distractions that take away from physical conditioning. These include the internet, smart phone texting, video games, and mega-channel television. Kids need to get outside and play often, and also get into team sports to socialize and compete. As an example, my son and daughter participated in swimming, gymnastics, soccer, and downhill skiing by the age of eight, and my son in football at age nine. They are both solid athletes with good balance and awareness thanks to the diversity of sports and activities they participated in.

Teen Athletes

If you are a teen age athlete, from middle school through high school, you are at the age where foundational strength should be developed through weight training and other resistance exercise such as body weight exercises, medicine balls, and resistance bands. You should be careful not to use shock methods like plyometrics until you have built a solid foundation of strength. Do not rush your development. Be consistent and focused on building a solid foundation and performance excellence will come. The base strength will allow you to develop more explosive traits as well and to later master sport specific skills.

The coaches I work with that train teen athletes often lament the fact that they get kids in high school that are physically unfit to play a sport well because they have no foundation of strength or athleticism, and it takes the coach a year or longer to build these traits, when they should have been built earlier such as in elementary and middle school.

Ergogenic supplement programs for teen athletes should help maximize training results while introducing a minimum number of nutrients such as protein supplements like whey protein, and in later teen years (high school) creatine and a few others you'll learn about. A low dose multivitamin supplement can be consumed as well as fish oil. Keeping ergogenic nutrition simple and focused at this period of development will be more effective than introducing a bunch of ingredients that create "metabolic noise" and diffuse the training effects. From my experience, any supplement plan that contains more than a few research proven ingredients is overkill and also may actually interfere with the adaptive response. I'll cover this in detail later in the book.

Athletes today are exposed to hundreds of different sport nutrition supplements, drinks, and bars. I have nothing against flavored electrolyte drinks or bars because they are a good source of fluids and calories. I do not see any ergogenic effects from these as they are made for the masses including fat old men sitting on their rider lawnmower during a hot summers afternoon of cutting the back yard, and girlfriends going on a casual hike in the hills. As for pushing the limits of athletic training and building explosive traits, they are really not very useful.

Most mass market drinks and bars are for mass market customers- heavily promoted to anyone with a pulse and supported with flashy ads and proper placement for the camera during post-game press conferences. There is nothing wrong with marketing, but a sales pitch is unproductive for the serious athlete focused on building explosiveness and sport specific skills.

Young Adult Athletes

If you are of college age or slightly older this is your time to really shine. Most elite and professional athletes go to college because that's where the scholarships, funding, exposure, and especially high level competitions are at. So that period between age 18 and 22 is a critical window of opportunity. Do not waste it.

By now you likely have built a solid foundation of strength and are working more on explosiveness and sport specific skills. Your training and competing with great explosiveness demands specialized training that, while not the focus of this book, should still be taken into account as this dictates what nutrients will help you amplify the adaptive result. When the right training and the right ergogenic nutritionals are combined, the results can be phenomenal.

Whenever I counsel athletes and coaches I always inquire as to what the athlete is doing in their training. Are they in a maximal strength building cycle? Are they doing shock training like plyometrics? Are they trying to lose excess body fat? Are they just trying to hang on and not get broken during a long competitive season?

Unless you know this you can never program a successful ergogenic nutrition plan to support the training and maximize the adaptive result. This is because Ergogenic nutrients in many cases are signaling molecules that turn on or off specific genes integral to the adaptive response. In a strength or muscle building cycle you want to maximally turn on specific anabolic gene pathways while at the same time taking care to dumb down the pathways that diffuse the muscle anabolic response. In contrast, if you or your athlete (if you are the coach) is focused on losing excess body fat, the athlete will need to switch on their fat burning genes.

Ergogenic nutrients are nutrigenomic, meaning they influence genes. If you introduce the right ergogenic nutrient(s) at the right time in the right dose, and likewise do not introduce the wrong nutrients, you will adapt optimally. If you introduce the wrong nutrients during the training cycle you may achieve no positive result and may even dis-adapt. This is why I always discourage athletes from consuming supplements that contain too many ingredients in them because, aside from marketing hype, looking more "complete" on the label and also costing more, they can easily interfere with the adaptive response to training- and this is a bad thing.

Working with an athlete I'd like to know their yearly plan as well as the macro and micro-cycles within the plan so I know which supplements will help maximize performance and gains at specific times. Ergogenic nutritional supplements are rarely consumed constantly over many training cycles. As the cycles change so must the ergogenic nutrients, so to maximize the specific adaptive response. The training leads the way and the ergogenic nutrients (as nutrigenomic triggers and metabolic master switches) amplify the result.

Athletes from a Soviet sport school. The Soviet system of athlete talent selection was very refined and a big reason for their huge success in international competition. Young athletes would leave home and live at the school where they would receive first class training. Brunner Photo.

Adults

When an athlete enters their middle 20's or beyond, hopefully they have evolved in their training so that they are now at an advanced level. Many athletes who end their college athletic career enter the workforce and detrain. But others at the top of their sport aspire for more victories, and perhaps a big paycheck. You may be one of the few who have set your sights on competing in the Olympics or perhaps a professional career. By now, if you are that elite you are most likely genetically and physically more fine-tuned for success in your sport than 99.9% of people on the planet. To succeed you will need to really dial in to your full potential abilities because those athletes you compete against are elite too.

Working with Olympians and pros in sports like football, baseball, basketball, track & field sprints, jumps, and throws, rowers, swimmers, road and sprint cyclists, and a handful of other athletes over the years has given me a great appreciation at just how metabolically fine-tuned they are. Elite athletes can react differently to ergogenic nutritionals than younger or less advanced athletes. Elite athletes often train differently and genetically respond differently to nutrients. For this reason it is imperative for the athlete to pay even stricter attention to what they put in their bodies, how much, and when. Diet and ergogenic nutrients can influence the training result both positively and negatively. You'll learn about this in sections to follow.

To measurably influence explosiveness and maximize the adaptation to training at the elite, Olympic and professional level is much harder to do than it is with less experienced athletes. But a 3-7% increase in performance at the elite level often results in extraordinary sporting results. Sometimes we see even greater improvements and it's almost always because we were able to tweak the training plan along with the addition of specialized supplements, to gain the specialized synergy necessary to make the leap. Inefficient nutrition or poor nutritional ergogenics can stall training, and when improvements are made the training intensity and/or volume can be elevated which synergistically results in superior gains.

Masters Athletes

There comes a time when old dogs long for the feeling of training and competition again and they reenter their previous sport or take up a new one. A major area of my research and training is working with older individuals, some athletes and some not so much. I'm talking about a man or women who are in their late 40's, and likely well beyond. It's harder for an older person to make gains in muscle, burn off excess body fat, and also build the strength and power necessary to compete. If it were easy we would see 70 year old men walking around looking like young Spartans or Gladiators- and we don't.

Older athletes have new challenges that I've found can often be overcome, but the training and the nutrition are quite different as they age. While this book is mainly written for younger athletes and their coaches, I know there are many of you older coaches or former athletes who are still training and may be competing as well, myself included. While I rarely throw the hammer any more, I do still put the shot put with the young track & field throwers I coach. Closing in on my 60's has allowed me to experiment on myself and also focus on the science of how to build muscle, strength, and power in seniors. I've dialed in on some useful training and nutrition science and applied this to training and it works well.

Message to Coaches

While it's common for smart young athletes to take charge of their diet and any ergogenic nutrition they may use, it's still very important for the coach to be in the loop. Restoration and adaptation to training stress does not occur unless the right environment is created in recovery, and this is where diet and supplements are most important. The vast amount of effort you and your athletes put in to training in the weight room, the gym, on the track or the field, and/or the pool can be wasted if adaptation does not occur. You will never get the time back. As a coach who wants his or her athletes to perform at their best, and to win, it's vital that you master ergogenic nutrition. This comes from a deeper understanding of what makes a great base diet and what ergogenic nutritional supplements will turn on adaptive gene pathways.

Training, diet, and ergogenic supplements must be in sync because it is their synergy that results in amazing improvements in explosive athletic ability. The best training with a lousy diet and no supplements will result in failure. Likewise the best diet and supplements with improper training will fail as well. It is all or nothing to create the ideal environment. That's why I often spend as much time with coaches discussing the training plan as I do planning supplement routines. Training as we all know is progressive: Baby steps followed by a plateau, then repeat. We all know it can take years to develop an elite athlete and careful course corrections as to training, diet, and ergogenics are necessary.

Final Thoughts

Of course, most competitive athletes are not elite. They are average kids in middle school, high school, or college that simply want to play, to be a part of something memorable. This does not mean that they should train haphazard, eat junk food, and slack off in training. Oftentimes, with young athletes, we coaches have to work with what we've got. Sometimes if you are skilled enough, and lucky enough, you can develop your program into a regional or national powerhouse.

I want to share a learning experience that I had. I trained in high school with a fellow football player named Bob Ladouceur. Bob went on to become a football coach at De La Salle High School in Concord, California at the young age of 25. From 1992 to 2004, as their head coach he guided the Spartans to 12-consecutive undefeated seasons, setting a national winning streak record for high school football of 151 consecutive wins. Bobs record is 399-25-3, with 17 California state championships and 7 national championships.

I've attended a few Spartan practices and games over the years and always marvel at how precise and with collective purpose the team trains and competes. Bobs athletes have not always been the most gifted, although he has had his share. They've all learned to train with focus and developed the foundation of strength and explosiveness as well as discipline necessary to excel. Bob has said that the most important person in his program is the Strength and Conditioning coach. The kids train in the weight room like they play on the field- with passion and focused purpose. The strength coach truly knows each player and is essential in helping mold them into a well-conditioned athlete.

If for one minute you think they don't address diet and supplement use at De La Salle you'd be greatly mistaken. These kids live and breathe the football program and that includes eating right and restoring correctly. Creating the optimal adaptive response from each workout is their goal. They do this year-round and they train just about every day.

As a coach, you are in a very powerful position to make change. Please take away all you can from this book about ergogenic nutrients, diet, and also what explosive athletes should never consume- so you can help develop all your athletes into amazing men and/or women that fully maximize their genetic gifts.

A Word for Team Trainers and Physicians

I feel it's important that team trainers and physicians are aware of what athletes are consuming in their diet and also their supplement protocol. Trainers and physicians encounter weight loss, hyperthermia, contusions, muscle, tendon and ligament strains and tears, sprains and bone breaks, and concussions. Diet and supplements can play a role in all these areas including getting the athletes back to health faster. If athletes do not restore properly they are more prone to injury, chronic fatigue, reduced motivation to train, and attention. It's important to understand how nutrients can prevent overtraining and also speed recovery from injury.

Rick Brunner hoists a kettlebell (well before they were popular in the USA) during a visit to a Russian gym during the summer of 1990. Good form, but lose the tie next time.

THE TRAINING-ERGOGENIC CONNECTION

Explosive athletic training is all about getting muscles to do more of what you want them to do in competition- to win. For athletes in events and sports that require explosive force this often means training your muscles to be more explosive. This occurs at the molecular level of cells. As such, exercise influences genes: It's Ex-ergenomic. Training-induced adaptations are reflected by changes in muscle contraction protein and function, mitochondrial function, metabolic regulation, intracellular signaling, and transcriptional response- in one very complex and interrelated package.

The well-established molecular (at the gene, DNA level) mechanisms that control adaptation to exercise training involve the gradual change in protein content and enzyme activity. These changes are comprised of activation and/or repression of signaling pathways that regulate protein transcription and translation as well as exercise –responsive gene expression. These include post-exercise changes in gene transcription involved in carbohydrate metabolism, fat mobilization, transport and oxidation, muscle regulators, and transcription regulators of mitochondrial biogenesis. The net effect is to promote optimal performance during future exercise challenge under enhanced resistance to fatigue.

Skeletal muscle comprises about 40% of the human body mass. All athletes are born with a unique ratio of slow twitch (ST) or Type I, and fast twitch (FT) or types IIa and IIx, muscle fibers based on the contraction properties of "time-to-peak tension" or "twitch" characteristics. These two main types of fibers combine to get the job done. ST fibers are endurance fibers. You'll see more of them in long-distance runners compared with the runners FT fibers. In Olympic Weightlifters you will find a larger number of FT fibers, necessary for short-burst explosive force.

Specific training can modify genetics by transforming muscle fibers, mostly from FT to become ST which are not as powerful but have greater endurance. Training can also be targeted at building larger FT fibers for explosive force. Most explosive sports are FT dominant and ST supportive, meaning the fast twitch muscle fibers are built for all explosive traits like speed, power, reaction, and striking force, but also have ST fibers to assist in maintaining the ability to repeat force such as speed-strength-endurance.

During exercise the contribution of various metabolic pathways to energy provision is determined by the intensity and power output of the exercise bout. This power output determines the rate of ATP demand and energy expenditure while the exercise intensity influences the relative contributions of carbohydrate and fat sources, and circulating and intramuscular fuel stores to provide energy.

At low-to-moderate exercise intensity the primary fuel sources to supply muscle are glucose from the liver or oral ingestion, and fats from adipose cells. Muscle glycogen is the primary carbohydrate during moderate to intense exercise. Phosphocreatine and finally ATP is the primary fuel source during the most intense explosive or short burst exercise.

Muscle protein synthesis (MPS) is the driving force behind adaptive responses to exercise. Research has shown that changing the exercise workload and intensity results in different outcomes. MPS is not achieved with resistance exercise at 20 to 40% of a single rep maximum but is maximal at 70 to 90% when the workload is matched (load x number of reps). New research has shown that low-intensity exercise done to failure maximizes the anabolic response as well.

There are three main subcellular fractions of proteins in muscle and these are myofibrillar, sarcoplasmic, and mitochondrial. These subcellular fractions are developed differently depending upon the types of exercise. Resistance exercise generally develops myofibrillar muscle while endurance exercise builds up sarcoplasmic and mitochondrial fractions. The successful adaptation to exercise in terms of an increase in muscle and improved performance depends upon the exercise imposed (e.g. force, reps, duration, volume, sequence, speed, etc.) as well as by the athletes genetic makeup which dictates their response ability.

In healthy athletes, skeletal muscle proteins have a turnover rate of about 1.2% each day and exist in dynamic equilibrium. In the fasted state muscle protein breakdown exceeds muscle protein synthesis, while in the fed state muscle protein synthesis exceeds breakdown. In response to exercise, muscle protein synthesis is increased for a time while muscle breakdown also increases or remains the same, depending on if nutrition is supplied in recovery. An increase in muscle protein synthesis drives adaptation to exercise training.

For many years research has shown that the acute response of muscle to resistance exercise in terms of muscle protein synthesis depended upon both workload and intensity. For intensities ≤ 40% of a single-rep maximum (1-RM) there are no detectible increases in muscle growth, whereas at intensities greater than 60% 1-RM, exercise increases muscle protein synthesis by 2- to 3-fold. However, recent research has shown that even resistance exercise of 30% 1-RM can yield similar rates of muscle protein synthesis as athletes training at 90% 1-RM, but only when the exercise is performed to failure and not when work is matched between 30 and 90% 1-RM. This means that increasing the volume of work at a lower intensity can overcome a blunted muscle protein synthesis, probably as a result of increased Type II muscle fiber recruitment due to the fatiguing nature of contractions. Introducing low-load fatiguing contractions may represent a feasible approach to stimulating muscle growth while avoiding the risk of injury when lifting heavy weights. This can be of use to young athletes, less experienced athletes, and master's athletes.

As athletes age they become anabolic resistant. Older athletes build much more muscle and strength through lower intensity resistance to failure, with double the volume; than they do trying to lift like a younger athlete would with a greater % of 1RM.

The anabolic response to resistance exercise is limited in duration. Immediately after exercise there is a latent period prior to muscle protein synthesis that is related to the intensity of exercise. The greater the intensity of the workout the longer the delay in muscle protein synthesis, up to as much as three hours post-exercise. After this latent period muscle protein synthesis rises sharply between 45 minutes and three hours and can be sustained for another hour if nutrition is not introduced in recovery (a fasted state). If essential amino acids are introduced in ample amounts in early recovery, muscle protein growth can be activated for upwards of 24 hours. So timing of nutrition and ergogenic supplements is important, yet not so much as originally believed, and the growth window can be large which means you should space your proteins and calories out over the full anabolic window which is several hours up to 24 hours.

As an athlete becomes more efficient in their training they accelerate their adaptive response. Research has shown that the duration of the anabolic response is shortened, likely due to a greater adaptive efficiency. Loaded resistance exercise results in increases in myofibrillar muscle proteins while unloaded endurance type exercise results in mitochondrial protein synthesis. This is very important to understand because how an athlete is trained dictates what type of muscle proteins they build. Since this book is directed to athletes that need to build explosiveness traits on a base of strength, it is essential for them to train in ways to activate neuromuscular power and not so much for extended endurance, except for when power-endurance (maintaining explosiveness) is important. This will depend upon the sport played or position of the athlete. For two extreme examples in explosive athletes, an Olympic weightlifter demands great explosive power for a very limited time, followed by a sizable rest period, while a football defensive lineman needs bursts of explosiveness (both lower and upper body at various angles) followed by short rest periods, over and over again for four quarters (and sometimes more in overtime) of a game.

Would you ever expect an Olympic lifter to need to run much distance? Of course not as this is not sport specific. Likewise, would you ever expect a football lineman to run much beyond five to ten yards for a few seconds during a game? Again, of course not. So why is it that in football a lineman often runs the same conditioning distances (wind sprints) as a wide receiver? The metabolic, physiologic, and neurologic demands in competition must be mimicked, even overstretched, in practice-specific to what the athlete must do in their sport.

While the effect of resistance exercise on muscle mass has long been recognized, the mechanisms underlying the link between high-resistance contractions and the regulation of protein synthesis and breakdown are, to date, poorly understood. Recent research has established that skeletal muscle is a "mechanosensitive" cell type, with the possible mechanisms through which mechanically-induced signaling events leading to changes in rates of protein synthesis. This is a process known as mechanotransduction which refers to the many mechanisms by which cells convert mechanical stimulus into chemical activity, driven especially by muscle contraction.

Joe Montana handing off to Roger Craig, running back for the three time Super Bowl champion San Francisco 49ers. A great era of Bay Area football and a pleasure for the author to be able to roam the field. Brunner Photo. November, 1988.

Contraction-Induced Signal Transduction Pathways in Exercised Muscle

Muscle contractions result in mechanical strain, ATP turnover, reactive oxygen and nitrogen species (RONS, aka free radicals), heat shock proteins (HSP), myokines (inflammatory and anti-inflammatory cytokines), and hypoxia (lack of oxygen). These have all been shown to activate signal transduction cascades regulating skeletal muscle adaptability. The signaling mechanisms are all essential to maximizing the adaptive response to training. While on the surface one would think that free radicals or inflammatory cytokines would be a negative influence on exercise and should be dealt with via antioxidants or anti-inflammatory NSAIDs, reducing them below their signaling zone can result in dis-adaptation and a poor sport result. This is not well known outside specific scientific circles, especially to athletes and coaches. I'll go into detail about these important signaling molecules in skeletal muscle plasticity and the adaptive response in following sections.

AMP-Activated Protein Kinase Signaling (AMPK)

AMPK is a master signaling enzyme that is increased in cells during reduced cell energy such as an increase in the AMP/ATP and Creatine/Phosphocreatine ratios. In addition to intense exercise, certain plant derived signaling compounds activate AMPK. Acute exercise increases AMPK phosphorylation (activation) and enzymatic activity dependent upon exercise intensity.

In general, AMPK activation acts to conserve ATP by inhibiting ATP hungry anabolic pathways such as skeletal muscle protein synthesis and glycogen synthesis driven by the growth regulating protein mTORC1, while increasing glucose transport (AMPK pathway improves insulin sensitivity) and fat metabolism (reduces fat) by increasing the number of mitochondria and their activity in cells. Mitochondria are organelles inside muscle cells that have their own DNA and are essential to cell energy. The greater the number of mitochondria and the more active they are, the greater the cells endurance efficiency.

The process of breaking down fat to use as fuel involves cutting up triglycerides, the storage form of fat, into glycerol and three fatty acids. The glycerol is converted into pyruvic acid in the cytoplasm and catabolized through the Citric Acid Cycle in the mitochondria. The fatty acids are catabolized by the addition of oxygen in the mitochondria to be entered into the Citric Acid Cycle as two-carbon fragments. For each two-carbon fragment of fatty acid produced by adding oxygen, the cell can generate 17 molecules of ATP. This is 1.5 times the energy production (when compared carbon to carbon) as with glucose. Although lipolysis generates more energy, it requires more oxygen and occurs much more slowly than equal carbohydrate metabolism. ATP is the universal energy carrier, involved in a wide range of energy transformations, including muscle contraction, building proteins, cognitive functions, etc.

The key signaling pathway regulating exercise/nutrient-induced building of muscle is known as the mammalian target of rapamycin or mTOR. It is mTOR that ultimately triggers the phosphorylation (activation) of multiple translational initiation factor substrates. Whoa now! We're talking "science-speak" here. OK, let me explain.

Most athletes and coaches don't know much about how proteins are formed from amino acids, so let me elaborate. There are two main processes to building a protein (skeletal muscle protein, enzymes, etc.). These are transcription and translation. Transcription is the first phase. This is where the genetic information in a cell's DNA is copied onto a recently made messenger RNA (mRNA) kind of like passing on a template to make something. The second phase is translation. This is where mRNA then directs the assembly of proteins on ribosomes (rRNA) with the help of transfer RNA (tRNA) which deliver single amino acids for use in manufacturing. So, transcription is making the template and translation is using this template to assemble specific proteins such as individual enzymes and also skeletal muscle proteins from single (free form) amino acids.

Bulgarian weightlifters squatting during a morning training session. It was not uncommon for these elite lifters to train 2 to 3 times a day in preparation for the ultimate goal of being an Olympic champion. These athletes trained with a very high level of intensity, often attempting max lifts during workouts. Because of this level of training their ergogenic nutrition plan had to be quite precise. Brunner Photo.

Lipolytic/Mitochondrial
AMPK Pathway

Anabolic
mTORC1 Pathway

Intermittent Fasting/Aerobic & HIIT Exercise	Nutrigenomics	Resistance Exercise/Muscle Contraction	Nutrigenomics
↓	Resveratrol	↓	Whey/EAA's
↓	Green Coffee	↓	Leucine/HMB
ATP	Green Tea	IGF-1	TMG
↓	Grape Seed	↓	Mg/K Orotate
AMP		PI3K	Phosphatidic Acid
↓		↓	Omega-3 FFA
AMPK		AKT	
↓		↓	
PGC-1α		mTORC1	

The two primary genetic pathways involved in athletic performance are the AMPK/PGC-1α pathway which increases the quantity and activity of mitochondria to utilize fats as fuel, and the anabolic mTORC1 pathway which increases muscle protein synthesis. Explosive athletes will mostly create an mTORC1 rich environment during training to build muscle mass, strength, and power. Intense muscle contractions under optimal loads and nutrients like whey protein and Phosphatidic acid listed above help to amplify the mTORC1 anabolic effect.

In some cell types, testosterone interacts directly with androgen receptors, whereas, in others, testosterone is converted by 5-alpha-reductase to dihydrotestosterone, an even more potent agonist for androgen receptor activation, an androgen-inducible member of the nuclear receptor superfamily of transcription factors.

The primary mechanism of action for androgen receptors is direct regulation of gene transcription. In molecular biology and genetics, a transcription factor is a protein that binds to specific DNA sequences, thereby controlling the flow (or transcription) of genetic information from DNA to messenger RNA. Transcription factors are protein complexes that help RNA polymerase bind to DNA. RNA polymerase is the enzyme that "transcribes" genes to make messenger RNA, which is then used to make proteins. By controlling RNA polymerase's access to the gene, transcription factors control the rate at which a gene is transcribed (a template is made of the gene). Without transcription factors, cells would not be able to effectively regulate the rate at which genes are expressed.

The media has become fixated on anabolic steroids (testosterone mimics) thinking they play an exclusive role in building muscle mass and strength. Nothing could be further from the truth. In many cases a lack of high testosterone is not the rate limiting factor in building muscle. This is one of the most important concepts you will read in this book, and a concept worth thinking about.

A rate limiting factor is some process that limits the outcome you seek. In my lectures and discussions with coaches and athletes I've often used the example of a highway that starts out as four lanes but then narrows to two lanes. Riding along in the four lanes the cars and trucks are going at the speed limit and beyond. But as the highway narrows to two lanes, the traffic slows way down and then stops and go's- in gridlock. The two lanes is an example of a rate limiting factor, that something that reduces efficiency and limits our end result or goal.

Now what if we were to expand the four lanes to six lanes. Would this improve efficiency? Perhaps a little by jamming the cars through, but not so much. It would likely increase the gridlock. Those six lanes would invite more drivers and entice them to drive fast. But suddenly they would come to a screeching halt as they come up on the two lanes. Tempers would flare; road rage would be brought out. No, the smart thing to do would be to expand the two lanes to four so that the entire road is four lanes of smooth driving. The rate limiting two-lane road would transform into a four-lane limitless road.

The same thing happens in our cells. Building explosive muscle that is efficiently linked to your nervous system and allows you to be a fine-tuned athlete is a highly complex process. To excessively focus on testosterone (or anabolic steroids) is naïve as this is rarely the rate limiting factor in making gains in explosiveness.

If you're an athlete, you are one anabolic shift from making a great leap in your performance. Likewise, as a Strength and Conditioning Coach, you are one shift from seeing more clearly the rate limiting pathways and how ergogenic nutrients can work with training to help your athletes boost performance.

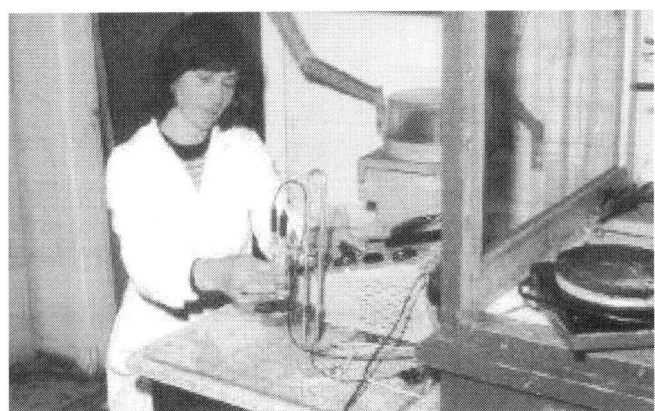

A Russian scientist at work in a Research Institue of Physical Culture in Leningrad in 1990. Since the 1960's the Institute was a major scientific facility challenged to investigate the use of nutrients in the anabolic and adapogenic processes of athletic performance. In the 1980's it was a major hub of anabolic steroid research. Today it houses the Sports Genetic Laboratory which studies gene polymorphisms in elite athletes in search of genes responsible for high value anaerobic and aerobic performance. Brunner Photo.

Skeletal Muscle Protein Synthesis via Contractions and Nutrient Stimuli

Intense muscle contractions build muscle by increasing mechanosensitive anabolic processes. During adaptation, muscle growth (hypertrophy) via protein translation and synthesis drives gains while the activation of satellite cells increase the ability to form myofibrils which increase muscle size.

Satellite cells lay dormant next to muscle fibers and divide during conditions of muscle damage or intensive muscle contractions. They then fuse with a muscle fiber to increase the number of myonuclei (and thus more DNA) to form more muscle. When athletes weight train for explosiveness they also increase neurological adaptations which favor increased muscle strength and power by improving motor unit activation, firing frequency, and sync of the high-threshold motor units.

Contraction stimulates the main anabolic pathway that has mTORC1 as its cornerstone. Muscle growth goes through mTORC1 and it is this enzyme that just may be the rate limiting factor in most training programs, and not testosterone as athletes often believe. The mTORC1 pathway controls mechanisms of muscle protein synthesis at many levels, especially translation of specific RNA's which end in muscle fiber enlargement.

Muscle growth via mTORC1 is also tied to both insulin and IGF-1 via the IGF-PI3K-

AKT-mTORC1 interaction. It is vital that muscle cells be sensitive to insulin so that insulin and IGF-1 can be leveraged to influence mTORC1 downstream. For most athletes, muscle sensitivity should not be a problem, as contractions improve sensitivity. However, if an explosive sport athlete is overfat, or of older age (generally age 50+), their muscles may be somewhat resistant to insulin due to excessive fats (e.g. saturated fats) and fat byproducts (e.g. ceramide) in muscle cells. This will blunt the anabolic response via reduced influence of IGF-1 on AKT, and mTORC1 will not be so active. To improve anabolic activity in overfat or older athletes they will need to burn the intramuscular fat (along with deep belly and liver fat) first, which will increase muscle sensitivity which then increases IGF-1 action toward increasing mTORC1.

An explosive athlete can achieve enhanced fat burning (lipolysis) without muscle mass and power loss by introducing high intensity interval training (HIIT) into their training cycles, more or less volume depending on how resistant (overfat muscle) they are. HIIT exercise accomplishes two things: it boosts the AMPK fat burning pathway very efficiently (increases quality and activity of mitochondria where fat is burned) while allowing the athlete to also turn on the mTORC1 pathway for muscle size and strength increase. HIIT is sizably more efficient and effective than traditional endurance exercise as it: (1) maintains a higher level of intensity of muscle contractions for strength and power maintenance; (2) boosts AMPK and PGC-1α efficiently; (3) takes much less time per workout to get beneficial results than long-distance aerobic exercise; and (4) is generally more forgiving on joints and connective tissue than higher volume endurance exercise.

Nutrient-Gene Interactions (Nutrigenomic) for Muscle Building and Fat Burning

The main focus of this book is on the building of an explosive athlete. This is an athlete that generally has the muscle mass and base strength to optimally perform their sport. An NFL Offensive lineman would obviously carry much more muscle mass and have a greater amount of base strength than would a professional tennis player. But both would want to move, react, and impart force necessary to overcome their opponent. Explosive muscle is the key to this. Building muscle that can move with precision and force are key traits of all explosive sports. So how do you amplify building this explosive muscle with ergogenic nutrition?

The following chapters outline five main sub-categories toward building muscle explosiveness. They list which nutrients specifically act as gene switches to influence the specific processes which are: anabolic (muscle building); energetic; lipolytic (fat burning); neurologic (nerve-muscle interaction); and adaptogenic (recovering from training stress). No single sub-category stands alone in building explosiveness because they are all interrelated.

Each individual athlete has a genetically predetermined capacity to respond or adapt to exercise training. Some athletes have genes which are more sensitive to nutrients while others are more blunted (nutrigenomic resistance or non-responders).

Randy Barnes, Shot Put indoor and outdoor (75' 10.25") world record holder, Olympic Silver (Seoul) and Gold (Atlanta) medal winner. Brunner Photo. Bruce Jenner Classic.

Nutrigenomic Anabolic Networks of Athlete Adaptation: Maximizing Muscle Mass, Strength, and Explosiveness

Building functional muscle that is explosive is about creating the right environment in muscle cells to grow and adapt to a higher level of intensity. Resistance training is used to build muscle mass, strength, and power. This resistance need not just be lifting weights as a number of resistance methodics can be used including resistance bands, medicine balls, body weight, parachutes and sleds, etc. Even electrical stimulation and muscle stretching can be utilized at times to stimulate muscle growth and power.

The goal of exercise is to create the right resistance and speed of resistance to change the metabolic environment in muscle and correct any rate limiting factors-to elicit an efficient adaptive change. As we discussed earlier, it is vital that various transcription and translation factors and signaling molecules, including the right balance of hormones, free radicals (RONS), heat shock proteins (HSPs), Calcium flux, pH (lactic acid), cytokines (IL-6, TNF-α), and cell energetics (ATP/AMP) be active in the right amount to stimulate muscle growth (via mTORC1) and neuromuscular response (the motor unit / increased force and reduced time of contraction). It is important to not interfere (e.g. the consumption of dis-adaptive nutrients) with these stress response proteins during exercise and in short-term recovery.

Your inherited muscle fibers determine the size potential of muscle fibers by setting their number, while environmental stimuli like training and nutrients that activate mTORC1 mainly regulate the size of muscle fibers. What is the relationship between muscle size and muscle protein anabolism? The size of muscle fibers, protein synthesis (anabolism) and breakdown (catabolism) are interrelated because proteins are the major component of muscle, with myosin, actin, and collagen accounting for about 85% of all protein-bound amino acids. Amino acids are continually being taken up to build muscle tissue anabolism and released because of catabolism. After intense resistance exercise, if the athlete were to not consume dietary protein for several hours, the restoration and anabolism of the muscle worked during exercise would have to pirate amino acids from other body protein sources including those proteins within the muscle cells. This is highly inefficient and rate limiting.

Muscle protein synthesis occurs mainly through extracellular amino acid availability combined with activation of the mTORC1 pathway- plus energy (i.e. ATP and PCr). Think of this as "parts plus assembly." Resistance training stimulates the mTORC1 pathway (assembly) while certain nutrients also influence this pathway. The goal of proper training programming along with the right nutrients, in the right amount, at the right time collectively should be focused on correcting any rate-limiting processes in the transcription-translation environment or setting (milieu).

Although DNA stores the information for protein synthesis, and RNA carries out the instructions encoded in DNA, most biological activities are carried out by proteins. The accurate synthesis of proteins is critical to the proper functioning of cells and athletic performance.

Testosterone interacts directly with androgen receptors. The primary mechanism of action for androgen receptors is direct regulation of gene transcription. Up-regulation or activation of transcription results in increased synthesis of messenger RNA, which, in turn, is translated by ribosomes to produce specific proteins. Messenger RNA (mRNA) carries the genetic information copied from DNA in the form of a series of three-base code "words," each of which specifies a particular amino acid. Transfer RNA (tRNA) is the key to deciphering the code words in mRNA. Each type of amino acid has its own type of tRNA, which binds it and carries it to the growing end of a polypeptide chain if the next code word on mRNA calls for it. Ribosomal RNA (rRNA) links with a set of proteins to form ribosomes. These are more complex structures which move along an mRNA molecule to assemble amino acids into protein chains.

So, now that the muscle cell has the "instructions" on how to build new proteins, be they hormones, enzymes, skeletal muscle protein, or collagen proteins (for tendons and ligaments) all we need now is to assemble proteins efficiently and have all the parts to do so. The entire package is: Instructions (Transcription) PLUS Parts and Assembly (Translation).

Rate limiting factors can occur at any point of the continuum, from Transcription (Testosterones influence OR poor mRNA number or activity for Instruction) or in Translation (Reduced number or activity of rRNA and tRNA) to influence Assembly, and/or amino acids as the Parts. Maximizing athletic adaptations demands uncovering rate limits and correcting for them, then addressing another one, and so on. By cleaning up the bottlenecks to muscle growth, strength, or explosiveness an athlete can excel to a new level. For most athletes a lack of ample testosterone is usually not the bottleneck. To introduce anabolic steroids into the training program of young athletes (i.e. younger than 45 years of age), while this "forces" anabolism, similar to expanding our highway from four lanes to six, it is not generally the most efficient way to improve performance (i.e. expanding the rate limiting two lanes to four).

So, let's now look at specific nutrients which can influence muscle in a nutrigenomic way by increasing the anabolic response via mTORC1 activation and protein translation.

BUILDING SKELETAL MUSCLE PROTEINS: THE PARTS AND THE ASSEMBLY

The following nutritional ergogenics are among my favorites for boosting muscle protein synthesis as well as the synthesis of adaptive enzymes and support proteins for explosiveness. While no single nutritional discussed is a be-all end-all in maximizing athletic performance, each can play a unique role in creating the synergy for performance enhancement.

PROTEIN

Every athlete and coach knows that protein from the diet is important in building muscle and that explosive athletes require more protein than a non-athlete. This protein can come from meat, fish, eggs, and dairy products, as well as from vegetable sources including seeds and nuts, rice and beans, and to a lesser extent from greens and berries. They all contain protein, some much more and some much less.

How much protein does an athlete need to consume in a day? That depends upon their age, level of fitness, and the training plan they are using. Common sense and scientific research suggest that the more strength training (volume, intensity, muscle groups) an athlete does, whereby there is a great increase in muscle contractions which not only degrade muscle via catabolism but also stimulate anabolism in recovery, will demand much more protein from the diet than a sedentary person.

The type of protein is important. Protein from meats like beef, lamb, chicken, and pork, as well as dairy and fish are more balanced for human muscle growth than vegetable proteins. But this should not deter athletes from eating vegetables, beans, seeds, and the like because they also contain valuable nutrients and non-nutrients (like polyphenols) that are important for health. The term "complete protein" refers to foods that have all nine essential amino acids present in the correct proportion for our bodies to build protein with. The term "incomplete protein" refers to foods which have all the essential amino acids, but are simply low in one or more of them. This is called the "limiting amino acid" and needs to be elevated by combining one deficient food with one rich in the limiting amino acid.

While it's true that most whole plant foods have one or more limiting amino acids and are thus "incomplete", this shouldn't send you running for a steak every time you need protein. If you're eating a good mix of vegetables, seeds, nuts, grains, beans and peas, and fruits, then your body simply collects what it needs from the "amino soup" that your digestion system has absorbed and makes available. There are a growing number of vegan bodybuilders, ultra-marathon runners and award-winning athletes out there to prove that meeting your protein needs on a plant-based diet is possible. However, with strength trained athletes who demand more protein, if they are vegan they may need to supplement additional vegetable derived protein in powder form.

As for how much protein an explosive athlete should consume in a day, there is no easy answer as there are many variables. However, even if an athlete goes overboard a bit the extra protein will simply be broken down and used as fuel. Unlike muscle glycogen or fatty acids, there is no big pool of amino acids just waiting around in the liver, belly, or muscle waiting to be used. Protein is all about timing and a dose the body can use to build at any one time.

I can only give you some examples to stimulate your thought process. Protein needs depend on what your sport demands from your muscles: What training cycle you are in (such as a muscle mass and strength cycle versus a competitive phase); how old you are (younger athletes require less protein than senior athletes); and what your experience is (more experienced athletes generally require less protein than novice athletes to grow- due to adaptive efficiencies) will dictate your protein needs.

In general, I recommend to the athletes I coach (young Football Players and Track and Field Throwers) a diet containing about 1 gram of protein for each pound of fat free muscle mass that athlete carries. This is just a starting point and I observe how the athlete is improving in muscle mass, strength, and/or explosiveness depending upon the mix between their training cycle (heavy lifting cycles need more protein), their recovery methodics, and their diet. It is an imperfect scientific observation but it works well.

If for example an athlete needs a gram of protein a day for each pound of fat free mass (FFM) they carry, let's work the math. Let's say our athlete weighs 200 pounds and, upon checking their body fat %, we see its 15%. Since we need fat free mass (skeletal muscle organs, heart, enzymes, hormones) only (fat doesn't need much protein) we take 1.0 and minus .15 (15%) to get .85 (85% FFM). Now take the athletes weight of 200 pounds times our FFM% of 85% to get a fat free mass of 170 pounds. If we need 1 gram for each pound of FFM we thus need 170 grams of protein each day to hit our goal. The athlete can monitor their diet to learn how much protein they are getting. This includes protein in the meals the athlete consumes plus any supplemental protein from the nutrition bars, powders, or ready to drink beverages the athlete consumes as a supplement.

I want to add that you should not become fixated on protein as the only thing diet wise to focus on. From my experience many athletes do not get enough total calories each day for maximum gains in muscle mass, strength, and explosiveness. Energy is needed for muscle contractions and total calories from carbohydrate, protein, and fat are very important to athletic performance. Having lots of major energy currencies (ATP and PCr) to spend on ramping up RNA translation means the athlete needs ample total calories to build muscle. How many total calories an athlete needs is relative to their training demands.

Example: Over the years I've noticed that many young football players lose weight and explosive strength during the season. Muscle weight loss often starts during two-a-days and never seems to rebound. But with proper preparation, and then maintenance during the competitive season, strength and muscle mass can actually be increased.

One thing that often happens is that athletes consume fewer calories than they need. There must be a sensible balance between high quality carbohydrates, proteins, and fats. Let's say our 200 pound athlete burns through 2,900 calories a day, which is realistic for their body weight and training intensity. Since we already determined that they will need 170 grams of protein each day, we simply multiply 170g times 4 calories per gram which supplies 680 calories (170g x 4 cal/gm). This is 23% of the 2,900 calories each day. Now we need to calculate carbohydrate and fat needs. Carbohydrate grams also contain 4 calories, while fat grams contain 9 calories. Let's estimate our needs for carbohydrate at 50% of calories (50% x 2,900 = 1,450 cal ÷ 4 cal/g = 362 grams of carbohydrate) and fat at 27% (27% x 2,900 = 783 cal ÷ 9 cal/g = 87 grams of fat).

Now, I don't know too many athletes or coaches, myself included that is this precise all the time with diet needs. If you have a starting point like this example which shows a need of around 170 grams of protein, 362 grams of carbohydrate, and 87 grams of fat, you can take a look at what you (or your athlete if you are a coach) are consuming from the diet and via dietary supplements (ready to drink shakes, powders, bars, and gels).

I have my protein ergogenic supplement favorites. I prefer to supplement with whey protein, either as an isolate or as a concentrate- doesn't seem to make much difference as long as the quality is very good. I don't get fancy with it.

Why whey protein? (1) It has a great profile of essential amino acids (EAA). EAA's are about half of all whey protein amino acids. They're the ones our body can't make from other amino acids, so they're essential. Ten grams of EAA's (in 20 grams of whey protein) are shown to maximally increase muscle protein synthesis in recovery from strength exercise. (2) Whey contains a greater amount of the branch chain amino acids (BCAA) leucine, isoleucine and valine. Most of you are familiar with BCAA's. It is now well accepted that leucine in particular acts as a powerful signaling molecule for muscle growth via the mTORC1 pathway. Whey has a bunch of leucine in it, about 2 grams in a 20 gram serving. (3) Whey tastes good and mixes well. Unlike many other protein powders, especially the vegetable derived proteins, whey is well liked by most athletes. (4) Whey is fast absorbed. Unlike casein (another dairy protein) and other proteins like egg or vegetable proteins, whey is absorbed faster. While this is not always a big deal, if you are consuming 20 grams of whey every 3-5 hours you want the protein to time right in this use window.

A quick word about the timing of protein, especially after exercise. Athletes have been told that they should consume protein immediately after exercise as the window for growth is short. Research has disproved this. In fact, if good protein sources are added to the diet at 3-5 hour intervals, this anabolic window will be 24 hours or longer. In fact, after exercise there is about a 30 to 90 minute lag in anabolism, depending on the stress of the workout, likely as the body trends from the catabolism of exercise to an anabolic process in recovery. Excessive lactic acid produced during training reduced pH and this pH needs to rise in recovery to stimulate anabolism. Knowing there is a transition from catabolism to anabolism, the first 20 to 25 gram dose of a protein supplement should be consumed between 30 minutes and 2 hours after the workout- and then every 3-4 hours thereafter.

Why 20-25 grams and not more? I've seen protein powders in some of the muscle stores that have doses of 30 grams and higher. That must be some big scoop. Recent research has shown that the body can utilize only about 10 grams of EAA, from 20 grams of whey protein, at any one time. This is known as the "muscle full" effect. The muscles cannot process more than about 10 grams of EAA in the anabolic pathway during each 3-4 hour period. What happens to the protein not used for muscle protein synthesis? It's used as fuel- very expensive fuel. Stick with close to a 20 gram serving size of whey and you won't go wrong. Monster sized athletes, like 320 pound NFL lineman and big weight throwers can increase their dose to 25-30 grams.

Researcher Michael Rennie from the UK, who in my opinion is one of the very top muscle protein research scientists in the world, has studied "muscle full" for some time. In a recent paper published in 2010, Rennie and his team write:

"The current results, together with those reported earlier demonstrated that, in response to a saturable quantity of AAs, after a latent period of '30–45 min, rates of myofibrillar and sarcoplasmic protein synthesis were increased for a period of '60–90 min before rapidly returning to basal rates, irrespective of the mode of AA delivery (i.e., oral protein compared with intravenous free AAs)."

"Note that the relatively short-term stimulation of MPS ('1.5 h), despite the continued AA availability, suggests that continuous intravenous nutrition is likely to result in the overprovision of AAs for protein synthesis."

In conclusion, mTORC1 signaling may control the increase in MPS after protein ingestion with the caveat that, if these signals indeed regulate increases in MPS to EAA, the functional significance of their outlasting MPS responses remains unexplained. Moreover, the short-term stimulation of MPS by AAs (at '1.5 h) suggests that optimal clinical strategies should involve pulse rather than continuous supply of AA.

Atherton PJ, Etheridge T, Watt PW, Wilkinson D, Selby A, Rankin D, Smith K, Rennie MJ. Muscle full effect after oral protein: time-dependent concordance and discordance between human muscle protein synthesis and mTORC1 signaling. Am J Clin Nutr. 2010 Nov; 92(5):1080-8.

I often add about 20 grams of whey to 1 to 1½ cups of chocolate milk. A cup of chocolate milk supplies 230 calories, containing 34 grams of carbohydrates, 10 grams of protein (80% casein proteins and 20% whey proteins), and 5 grams of fat. This whey fortified shake supplies 30 grams of total protein which includes 22 grams of whey proteins and 8 grams of casein proteins. I also sometimes add 20 grams of whey protein to a shake consisting of coconut water, milk, a banana, and strawberries. This way I get the protein as well as a good dose of potassium. I never buy flavored whey because I find the unflavored pure whey to be a better value and more flexible to my liking, as I can add whatever I want with it.

If you are drinking whey with milk you can back off on the dose a bit since milk has 80% casein and 20% whey. Casein is slower acting than whey. It takes longer to digest, while whey absorbs faster and also has a different amino acid profile. Casein is sticky which slows its absorption.

All protein supplements have value, be they animal or vegetable based, because all proteins contain amino acids in various ratios. Therefore, if you prefer to supplement with casein, egg, milk protein concentrate, or even fish protein, each will have benefits. As for vegetable based proteins, today there are many options to choose from. Just a few years ago there was pretty much only soy protein. Then rice protein it the market, followed by pea and hemp proteins. Vegetable based proteins don't have much leucine so I recommend a leucine supplement of perhaps 3 grams a serving to help boost mTORC1.

THE AMAZING BRANCHED-CHAIN AMINO ACID L-LEUCINE

L-Leucine is the king of amino acids as it is a powerful signaling compound for the main anabolic pathway mTORC1 (more properly the PKB/mTORC1/p70S6 kinase pathway). L-Leucine is the main BCAA and is an essential amino acid, meaning you must get it from foods or supplements.

How does l-leucine activate mTORC1? Some researchers speculate that l-leucine supplies energy directly to muscle in the form of elevated ATP. Leucine and the two other BCAA's function within a distinct pathway. BCAA's are not degraded in the liver due to the absence of branched-chain amino acid aminotransferase (BCAT) which is an enzyme that breaks down the BCAA's. While other amino acids are broken down in the liver, BCAA's survive to be delivered right to muscle. In muscle there is the BCAT enzyme which reduces the BCAA's to supply energy which lowers AMPK while raising mTORC1.

Recall that AMPK, which is a catabolic enzyme tied to mitochondria activity, is the counterbalance to mTORC1 which is anabolic. While both AMPK and mTORC1 are always present no matter what type of training you do (they do work together as a system), during heavy resistance training, when a maximal anabolic state for muscle growth, strength and power is the goal, you want to target mTORC1. This will simultaneously down-shift AMPK.

Of note is the influence of leucine on mitochondrial growth and activity. In general AMPK leads to Peroxisome proliferator-activated receptor gamma coactivator 1-alpha (PGC-1α), a protein transcriptional co-activator that regulates genes involved in energy metabolism. Because PGC-1α ramps up the ability of mitochondria to process energy, especially the use of fat as fuel, it is necessary for long-term repetitive explosive athletic performance. Explosive muscle needs fuel to function. In the short span this fuel is the immediate ATP and phosphocreatine (PCr) stores in muscle. But over longer periods such as repeated bouts of explosive effort, the muscle will look for optional fuels. Like a hybrid car that runs on gasoline and battery power, muscle cells can pull from various fuels too. The easier muscle can use a fuel the easier it is to maintain maximal effort.

During explosive team sports like football, basketball, soccer, and hockey which utilize short bursts of effort followed by a rest or downshift in effort, the main fuels are anaerobic such as ATP, PCr and even lactate. But some degree of aerobic fuel use is also present- to spare the anaerobic fuels for maximal explosiveness. This is where mitochondria come into play as they pull the energy out of fatty acids for use in muscle cells. The more mitochondria and the more active they are the more efficient this process is.

One study by Italian scientists found that while BCAA's enhanced mTORC1, they also had a positive influence in PGC-1α activity in mitochondria (mitochondrial gene expression).

Valerio A, D'Antona G, Nisoli E. Branched-chain amino acids, mitochondrial biogenesis, and healthspan: an evolutionary perspective. Aging (Albany NY). 2011 May;3(5):464-78.

An interesting study worth noting was one conducted by Michael Rennie and Paul Greenhaff from the UK. Considering the use of BCAA's as anabolic signaling molecules they looked at the dose response between amino acid availability and muscle protein synthesis and made some interesting discoveries. Here are some of their findings:

"The results of the first study (22) were somewhat of a surprise. We designed the study to allow us to make measurements of MPS before and during the infusion of mixed AAs over a period of 6 h. There appeared to be a latent period of about one-half hour before any increase in incorporation of AAs could be measured, but then there was a rapid and rather large stimulation of protein synthesis—somewhat larger than we had previously obtained when making measurements over periods of about 4–6 h. We also observed something that in retrospect seems obvious, i.e., that MPS turned off after about 2 h despite the continued availability of AAs, returning to basal postabsorptive values. In fact, it now seems that the behavior of muscle in the presence of exogenous AAs was similar to that predicted by Joe Millward (23) in suggesting that there was an upper limit to the amount of protein that could be contained within the muscle at a given time, determined ultimately by the muscle RNA:protein ratio and the connective tissue extracellular three-dimensional network."

"The implications of our findings are interesting in three ways: First, the results suggest that there must be a desensitization of the signaling mechanism that senses and transmits information concerning the availability of AAs; second, it would seem that long-term infusions of parenteral AA containing solutions are unlikely to maintain an anabolic effect beyond a couple of hours and that any AA not taken into tissue protein will simply be catabolized to urea. Last, it seems that, in the future, if accurate values of human MPS are to be obtained, then studies need to be confined to periods of 3 h, with 2.5 h seeming to be optimal; values obtained during studies of 4–6 h and longer periods are likely to be wrong."

"In the latter studies, we showed clearly that administration of exogenous AAs stimulated changes in phosphorylation of elements of the mammalian target of rapamycin (mTOR) pathway with increases in phosphorylation of mTOR itself and of the p70 ribosomal subunit S6 kinase (p70 S6 kinase) and eukaryotic initiation factor 4 binding protein 1 (eIF4 BP1) with relatively small doses of EAAs—10 g (25). The Boirie group (26) were also able to obtain evidence of stimulation of this pathway with a combination of hyperinsulinemia and hyperaminoacidemia, but our studies were carried out at concentrations of insulin that were clamped at 10 mU/mL, suggesting that, as we had previously hypothesized, large increases in insulin were not required for an anabolic stimulation of MPS by AAs."

Rennie MJ, Bohé J, Smith K, Wackerhage H, Greenhaff P. Branched-chain amino acids as fuels and anabolic signals in human muscle. J Nutr. 2006 Jan;136(1 Suppl):264S-8S.

What the above research suggests is that BCAA's and l-leucine in particular do act as signaling molecules to stimulate muscle growth, and they do so in a narrow window lasting under three hours, with an initial post-exercise period of inaction lasting about 30 minutes. The researchers recommend a pulse of amino acids. This is where consuming 20 grams of whey protein between 30 minutes and one hour, and then every three hours thereafter up to perhaps 3 doses (30 min post-exercise, hour 3, and hour 6), can be maximally anabolic.

Most explosive athletes still train to build mixed metabolic efficiencies. Of course there is some need of a certain amount of muscle mass and maximal strength for specific sports. Then this muscle must be made more responsive which requires the integration of the muscle cells with the motor units (neuromuscular response) as well as central nervous system synchronicity to maximize explosive force when needed. Therefore, the use of l-leucine, BCAA's, and even whey protein high in BCAA's is most important for use during high intensity high load resistance training cycles where maximum muscle size, strength, and explosiveness are the focus.

I repeat- during these training cycles it can be an advantage to consume these supplemental whey proteins, rich in BCAA's, at a dose of 20 to 25 grams starting one half to an hour after the workout, and then every 3 hours thereafter. If the athlete resistance trains twice a day, protein can become an even greater advantage in driving muscle protein translation and elongation as a part of the anabolic/restorative process, especially when used with other anabolic ergogenic nutrition to be discussed in following sections.

Also keep in mind that there are other variables involved that may influence the efficiencies of BCAA and whey in the anabolic process. This includes the fitness level of the athlete and their age. Older athletes who are anabolic resistant to muscle growth will likely need to strength train with greater volume (lower % of 1RM such as 50-60% for high reps to failure) along with a greater amount of EAA's and leucine, perhaps 30 to 40 grams of whey protein (15g to 20g of EAA's) and perhaps some supplemental leucine as 2 extra grams every 3-4 hours post-workout to build sizable muscle mass and strength.

Your author during one of many trips to Russia. Great memories of attending research institues in Moscow and Leningrad to learn from some of the best sport scientists in the world. Brunner Photo.

THE L-LEUCINE METABOLITE HMB

A major focus of nutrition after exercise is to maximize the anabolic shift in muscle protein balance. This is driven by a brief (about 2 hours) but sizable (3X) after-nutrition increase in muscle protein synthesis and a small (about 50%) contribution of muscle protein breakdown depression. Recent research has uncovered new biologically active nutrients that can, as anti-catabolic and anabolic triggers, assist in restoration and adaptation from training. One such nutrient is a metabolite of L-Leucine called β-hydroxy-β-methylbutyrate (HMB).

According to protein researcher Daniel Wilkinson from the University of Nottingham in the UK, as a branched-chain amino acid (BCAA), Leucine converted in muscle by the enzyme branched-chain aminotransferase to α-ketoisocaproate (α-KIC) before again changing by the mitochondrial enzyme branched-chain α-ketoacid dehydrogenase, then finally forming Acyl-CoA derivatives and entering the citric acid cycle. That's a lot of scientific words I know, but what it simply means is that Leucine is converted a few times and scientists are just now discovering that some of these metabolites may in fact be a more anabolic (increasing mTORC1) form. Additionally, an alternative metabolic fate for Leucine has been shown wherein the enzyme α-KIC dioxygenase found in muscle, liver, and kidney generates β-hydroxy-β-methylbutyrate (HMB) from Leucine.

"Orally consumed 3.42 g free-acid (FA-HMB) HMB (providing 2.42 g of pure HMB) exhibited rapid bioavailability in plasma and muscle and, similarly to 3.42 g Leu, stimulated muscle protein synthesis (MPS; HMB +70% vs. Leu +110%). While HMB and Leu both increased anabolic signalling (mechanistic target of rapamycin; mTOR), this was more pronounced with Leu (i.e. p70S6K1 signalling 90 min vs. 30 min for HMB). HMB consumption also attenuated muscle protein breakdown (MPB; -57%) in an insulin-independent manner. We conclude that exogenous HMB induces acute muscle anabolism (increased MPS and reduced MPB) albeit perhaps via distinct, and/or additional mechanism(s) to Leu."

Wilkinson DJ, Hossain T, Hill DS, Phillips BE, Crossland H, Williams J, Loughna P, Churchward-Venne TA, Breen L, Phillips SM, Etheridge T, Rathmacher JA, Smith K, Szewczyk NJ, Atherton PJ. Effects of leucine and its metabolite β-hydroxy-β-methylbutyrate on human skeletal muscle protein metabolism. J Physiol. 2013 Jun 1;591(Pt 11):2911-23.

Alway SE, Pereira SL, Edens NK, Hao Y, Bennett BT. β-Hydroxy-β-methylbutyrate (HMB) enhances the proliferation of satellite cells in fast muscles of aged rats during recovery from disuse atrophy. Exp Gerontol. 2013 Sep;48(9):973-84.

In a study by researchers in Brazil (Pinheiro, 2012), where rats were fed HMB, the authors write "No change was observed in time to peak of contraction and relaxation time. Resistance to acute muscle fatigue during intense contractile activity was also improved after HMB supplementation. Glycogen content was increased in both white (by fivefold) and red (by fourfold) portions of gastrocnemius muscle. HMB supplementation also increased the ATP content in red (by twofold) and white (1.2-fold) portions of gastrocnemius muscle. CS activity was increased by twofold in red portion of gastrocnemius muscle. These results support the proposition that HMB supplementation have marked change in oxidative metabolism improving muscle strength generation and performance during intense contractions."

Pinheiro CH, Gerlinger-Romero F, Guimarães-Ferreira L, de Souza-Jr AL, Vitzel KF, Nachbar RT, Nunes MT, Curi R. Metabolic and functional effects of beta-hydroxy-beta-methylbutyrate (HMB) supplementation in skeletal muscle. Eur J Appl Physiol. 2012 Jul;112(7):2531-7.

In a mouse study, HMB was shown to improve body composition and sensorimotor function during normal training and stopped muscle mass and strength loss during fat loss (catabolic conditions).

Park BS, Henning PC, Grant SC, Lee WJ, Lee SR, Arjmandi BH, Kim JS. HMB attenuates muscle loss during sustained energy deficit induced by calorie restriction and endurance exercise. Metabolism. 2013 Jul 19. pii: S0026-0495(13)00186-8.

In a recent paper, Jose Antonio, Richard Kreider and others wrote of the position stand of The International Society of Sports Nutrition (ISSN) on HMB. This stand outlined HMB's usefulness and also its use scheme.

"Position Statement: The International Society of Sports Nutrition (ISSN) bases the following position stand on a critical analysis of the literature on the use of beta-hydroxy-beta-methylbutyrate (HMB) as a nutritional supplement. The ISSN has concluded the following. 1. HMB can be used to enhance recovery by attenuating exercise induced skeletal muscle damage in trained and untrained populations. 2. If consuming HMB, an athlete will benefit from consuming the supplement in close proximity to their workout. 3. HMB appears to be most effective when consumed for 2 weeks prior to an exercise bout. 4. Thirty-eight mg·kg·BM-1 daily of HMB has been demonstrated to enhance skeletal muscle hypertrophy, strength, and power in untrained and trained populations when the appropriate exercise prescription is utilized. 5. Currently, two forms of HMB have been used: Calcium HMB (HMB-Ca) and a free acid form of HMB (HMB-FA). HMB-FA may increase plasma absorption and retention of HMB to a greater extent than HMB-CA. However, research with HMB-FA is in its infancy, and there is not enough research to support whether one form is superior. 6. HMB has been demonstrated to increase LBM and functionality in elderly, sedentary populations. 7. HMB ingestion in conjunction with a structured exercise program may result in greater declines in fat mass (FM). 8. HMB's mechanisms of action include an inhibition and increase of proteolysis and protein synthesis, respectively. 9. Chronic consumption of HMB is safe in both young and old populations."

Wilson JM, Fitschen PJ, Campbell B, Wilson GJ, Zanchi N, Taylor L, Wilborn C, Kalman DS, Stout JR, Hoffman JR, Ziegenfuss TN, Lopez HL, Kreider RB, Smith-Ryan AE, Antonio J. International Society of Sports Nutrition Position Stand: beta-hydroxy-beta-methylbutyrate (HMB). J Int Soc Sports Nutr. 2013 Feb 2;10(1):6.

In a human performance study, athletes consumed 3 grams of HMB in free acid form daily while following a high volume resistance training protocol. HMB reduced muscle protein breakdown (catabolism) after exercise and improved a perceived readiness to train. HMB had no influence on free testosterone, cortisol, or c-reactive protein (a marker of inflammation response).

Wilson JM, Lowery RP, Joy JM, Walters JA, Baier SM, Fuller JC Jr, Stout JR, Norton LE, Sikorski EM, Wilson SM, Duncan NM, Zanchi NE, Rathmacher J. β-Hydroxy-β-methylbutyrate free acid reduces markers of exercise-induced muscle damage and improves recovery in resistance-trained men. Br J Nutr. 2013 Aug 28;110(3):538-44.

In a rat study, researchers discovered that HMB treatment increased the content of pituitary Growth Hormone (GH) and GH mRNA, hepatic IGF-I mRNA and serum IGF-I concentration. No changes were detected on skeletal muscle IGF-I and myostatin mRNA expression. The HMB fed rats, although normoglycemic, exhibited hyperinsulinemia. Increasing growth hormone is an interesting finding. Hyperinsulinemia while of concern in older individuals who are insulin resistant are likely not of concerned to a younger well-trained athlete and may in fact contribute toward HMB's anabolic effects.

Gerlinger-Romero F, Guimarães-Ferreira L, Giannocco G, Nunes MT. Chronic supplementation of beta-hydroxy-beta methylbutyrate (HMβ) increases the activity of the GH/IGF-I axis and induces hyperinsulinemia in rats. Growth Horm IGF Res. 2011 Apr;21(2):57-62.

In a research paper by Steve Nissen and Rick Sharp a decade ago the scientists wrote "Creatine and beta-hydroxy-beta-methylbutyrate (HMB) were found to significantly increase net lean mass gains of 0.36 and 0.28%/wk and strength gains of 1.09 and 1.40%/wk (P < 0.05), respectively."

Nissen SL, Sharp RL. Effect of dietary supplements on lean mass and strength gains with resistance exercise: a meta-analysis. J Appl Physiol. 2003 Feb; 94(2):651-9.

HMB found its way into the mass supplement market when the pharmaceutical giant Abbott laboratories added it as their trademarked brand Revigor® to products in its aging care (Ensure®) and bodybuilding/fitness (EAS®) lines. I believe explosive athletes will also benefit from HMB.

Initially I was skeptical of HMB, not because it doesn't work but because it's pricier than L-Leucine. I'm always looking for value (benefit/cost ratio) of nutritionals. I reviewed the HMB science (animal and human) from the past 15 years and communicated with some of the primary HMB researchers without financial ties to HMB. I also reviewed the research and patents of those financially tied to HMB including early patent holder Steve Nissen and patent assignees Iowa State University and Abbott Laboratories. I'm not against a scientist conducting useful research and also benefiting from this research by receiving patent protection for thier efforts. Scientists and financial sponsors should benefit from their creativity and discovery of useful nutritionals because this can help athletes improve their performance.

Speaking with scientists involved in the HMB research, as well as reviewing all the published the human science, it seems that taking HMB before exercise in a dose of around 1 to 2 ½ grams, and then a similar dose an hour after exercise, should create a good anabolic (mTORC1) effect.

Pimentel GD, Rosa JC, Lira FS, Zanchi NE, Ropelle ER, Oyama LM, Oller do Nascimento CM, de Mello MT, Tufik S, Santos RV. β-Hydroxy-β-methylbutyrate (HMβ) supplementation stimulates skeletal muscle hypertrophy in rats via the mTOR pathway. Nutr Metab (Lond). 2011 Feb 23; 8(1):11.

Portal S, Eliakim A, Nemet D, Halevy O, Zadik Z. Effect of HMB supplementation on body composition, fitness, hormonal profile and muscle damage indices. J Pediatr Endocrinol Metab. 2010 Jul;23(7):641-50.

Eley HL, Russell ST, Baxter JH, Mukerji P, Tisdale MJ. Signaling pathways initiated by beta-hydroxy-beta-methylbutyrate to attenuate the depression of protein synthesis in skeletal muscle in response to cachectic stimuli. Am J Physiol Endocrinol Metab. 2007 Oct;293(4):E923-31.

CREATINE MONOHYDRATE

I'm a purest when it comes to creatine. I began using creatine monohydrate in athlete training cycles back in 1988. Originally I purchased the material from Pfanstiehl (Who no longer makes creatine monohydrate) and found the quality to be excellent. Back then the cost was between $70 and $100 a kilogram (2.2 pounds). The price today has dropped a ton. A high quality creatine monohydrate I prefer is manufactured by AlzChem AG in Germany under the Creapure® brand. It is the only creatine I recommend.

Many sport nutrition companies purchase creatine monohydrate from China manufacturers and suppliers, as well as market various non-monohydrate forms, but I have not been very happy with these and the results are either equal to the monohydrate form (at a higher cost) or less productive.

There is absolutely nothing wrong with the less expensive pure creatine monohydrate form as it has close to 100% absorption. I have also not seen any independent research that has shown other variations to be superior to the monohydrate form. In fact, research has shown some of these newer forms to be ineffective and potentially toxic. The reason many of these new variations are made and promoted is not so much for the athletes benefit, but to create a marketing distinction or high priced proprietary edge for the maker- definitely not a good value for the athlete. Today a season's supply of high quality creatine monohydrate should cost an athlete around $15 to $20.

Creatine is a low molecular weight amino acid derivative derived from the amino acids arginine, glycine, and methionine. The body makes a couple of grams a day, mainly in the kidneys, pancreas, and liver. The total pool in the body is about 140 grams. This is restocked from animal foods like red meats from the diet (about 1 gram/day) as well as made by the body. Vegetarian athletes are low in muscle creatine stores and should supplement with creatine monohydrate.

Eric Hultman from Sweden, and Roger Harris and Paul Greenhaff from the UK were the first scientists from outside the East Block to hone in on creatine monohydrate use in exercise. They were interested in the role of phosphocreatine in fatigue during intense muscle contractions. While Soviet athletes had used creatine in various forms prior to 1988, when Soviet scientists introduced me to it, it was not until Hultman, Harris, and Greenhaff published about creatine monohydrate in western journals that the athletic world began to take notice. Then information about creatine monohydrate hit the mass media, especially the bodybuilding magazines, and the rest is history.

A decade ago I was giving a lecture to a college football team and I was surprised at how few of them were using creatine. In a room of about sixty athletes I counted just a few users of creatine. Today more athletes are aware of creatine and its benefits but I find many still in the dark as to how it should be used properly, with which supplements it should be stacked (complexed), what types of conditioning cycles to use it in, and for how long. I'll answer some of these questions, but first let's take a look of what creatine monohydrate can do.

A main benefit to creatine is that it can replenish depleted creatine stores in muscle, especially Type II explosive fibers which are easily depleted during high-intensity sports. Creatine is stored as phosphocreatine (PCr) in muscle for use during anaerobic demands such as repetitive explosive force. Force requires adenosine triphosphate (ATP) as the energy source, and when it is depleted to AMP, force is reduced. PCr resupplies AMP with phosphate groups for maximum power. Muscle force is especially important to maintain sprinting power and creatine can enhance such power in a single sprint by 5% and during multiple sprints, such as during a football game, by up to 10%.

Creatine has also been found to increase cell volume as well as muscle glycogen levels. As such it is both anabolic and energetic in function.
In regard to power output and fatigue, a group of Australian researchers write:

"Repeated-sprint exercise provides an interesting model to investigate the mechanisms governing the decline in power output during whole-body, high-intensity dynamic activities which require high contraction rates similar to those encountered in many athletic activities. The majority of the energy required for all-out sprinting is derived from phosphocreatine (PCr) hydrolysis and anaerobic glycolysis, and repeated sprints therefore result in large changes in both PCr and hydrogen ion (H+) concentration. There is also an increased aerobic contribution when sprints are repeated but, nonetheless, even the latter sprints in a repeated-sprint bout remain predominantly anaerobic. Accordingly, most previous explanations of fatigue during repeated-sprint exercise have focused on factors associated with cellular muscle fatigue. These include limitations in anaerobic energy supply from adenosine triphosphate (ATP) and PCr and intramuscular accumulation of selected metabolic by-products including inorganic phosphate (Pi) and H+."

"While a correlation between PCr resynthesis and the recovery of single-sprint performance has previously been reported, we report for the first time that there is a significant correlation between the resynthesis of PCr and the recovery of repeated-sprint performance."

Mendez-Villanueva A, Edge J, Suriano R, Hamer P, Bishop D. The recovery of repeated-sprint exercise is associated with PCr resynthesis, while muscle pH and EMG amplitude remain depressed. PLoS One. 2012;7(12):e51977.

What this means to athletes is that the refilling of the phosphocreatine (PCr) pool is essential to maintain force and reduce fatigue during multiple efforts of explosive exercise. This would include athletes like lineman in football during a game, basketball players, rowers (crew), track sprinters in multiple heats, tennis players, and athletes in many more repetitive effort sports.

Creatine has an influence on anabolic gene expression. Mark Tarnopolsky from McMaster University in Canada (one of the leading scientists studying the effects of creatine monohydrate) along with researchers from Deakin University in Australia and the Buck Institute for Research on Aging in the USA published results of a useful human study using a loading phase of 20 grams of creatine monohydrate each day for three days followed by a maintenance phase using 5 grams daily for seven days. In a randomized, placebo-controlled, double-blind crossover protocol the creatine monohydrate cycle showed that participants significantly increased fat-free mass, total body water, and body weight.

One major finding was in regard to osmoregulation (cell swelling) which activates genes in osmosensing and signal transduction, cell remodeling, protein and glycogen synthesis, glucose transport (GLUT-4), satellite cell growth and activity, and DNA replication and repair. Most importantly, genes involved in RNA processing and transcription are activated. The authors conclude their paper by stating:

"We propose that CrM supplementation induces rapid and coordinate induction of these regulatory proteins at the molecular level, resulting in increases in maximal muscle strength and power, FFM, total body water, and total body weight, independent of training and/or dietary intervention."

Safdar A, Yardley NJ, Snow R, Melov S, Tarnopolsky MA. Global and targeted gene expression and protein content in skeletal muscle of young men following short-term creatine monohydrate supplementation. Physiol Genomics. 2008 Jan 17;32(2):219-28.

Athletes often ask when the best time to consume creatine is. I don't think it makes much difference. I've never recommended creatine pre-workout but have recommended morning consumption (if trainings are later in the day) or post-workout. I oftentimes combine 5 grams of creatine monohydrate with whey protein and consume this 30 minutes to one hour after the workout. If done consistently this seems to be quite anabolic. Research by Jose Antonio and Victoria Ciccone seem to support post-workout consumption as being superior.

Antonio J, Ciccone V. The effects of pre versus post workout supplementation of creatine monohydrate on body composition and strength. J Int Soc Sports Nutr. 2013 Aug 6;10(1):36. E-published ahead of print.

While most of the time athletes and coaches think of creatine as being energetic or anabolic, I believe there is a case for it being neurologic too. In another Australian study, researchers gave creatine to 45 young adults and looked at whether or not creatine would enhance intelligence test scores and working memory performance. The authors concluded that "Creatine supplementation had a significant positive effect (p < 0.0001) on both working memory (backward digit span) and intelligence (Raven's Advanced Progressive Matrices), both tasks that require speed of processing. These findings underline a dynamic and significant role of brain energy capacity in influencing brain performance."

Rae C, Digney AL, McEwan SR, Bates TC. Oral creatine monohydrate supplementation improves brain performance: a double-blind, placebo-controlled, cross-over trial. Proc Biol Sci. 2003 Oct 22;270(1529):2147-50.

In a study published way back in 2000, Jeff Stout, Joel Cramer and others found that 20 grams of creatine monohydrate daily for five days delayed the onset of fatigue in 15 college age women athletes.

Stout J, Eckerson J, Ebersole K, Moore G, Perry S, Housh T, Bull A, Cramer J, Batheja A. Effect of creatine loading on neuromuscular fatigue threshold. J Appl Physiol. 2000 Jan;88(1):109-12.

In a follow-up study in 2007, Cramer and Stout wrote:

"Previous studies have demonstrated increases in peak torque (PT) and decreases in acceleration time (ACC) after only 2 days of resistance training, and other studies have reported improvements in isokinetic performance after 5 days of creatine supplementation. Consequently, there may be a combined benefit of creatine supplementation and short-term resistance training for eliciting rapid increases in muscle strength, which may be important for short-term rehabilitation and return-to-play for previously injured athletes."

This study of twenty-five men in their early twenties found that creatine increased peak torque by 13% versus 6% for the placebo while the decrease in acceleration time (faster acceleration) improved by 42% versus 34% in placebo.

Cramer JT, Stout JR, Culbertson JY, Egan AD. Effects of creatine supplementation and three days of resistance training on muscle strength, power output, and neuromuscular function. J Strength Cond Res. 2007 Aug;21(3):668-77.

Creatine may also help to restore brain function after a concussion. In a recent study, eleven athletes who had each suffered a concussion showed a decrease in cerebral creatine levels. This provokes a longer time for normalization of metabolism, as well as longer time for resolution of concussion-associated clinical symptoms.

Vagnozzi R, Signoretti S, Floris R, et al. Decrease in N-acetylaspartate following concussion may be coupled to decrease in creatine. J Head Trauma Rehabil. 2013 Jul-Aug;28(4):284-92.

The standard protocols for using creatine monohydrate is to either load it for 5 days at a 5 gram dose, four times a day (20g/day), to quickly raise the level of muscle PCr, or consume just 5 grams per day over a longer period of time, perhaps a couple of weeks before PCr is saturated. For some athletes, consuming creatine monohydrate with some high glycemic carbs like glucose, sucrose, or branched chain maltodextrins may improve absorption.

While I generally recommend adding creatine monohydrate to chocolate milk with 20g of whey protein I also leave up to the athlete to get creative and consume what their personal tastes dictate and that they will enjoy drinking. Creatine is tasteless and mixes well so even a carbohydrate drink or mixed in water will suffice.

Research and practical use have shown that a small percent of athletes do not receive much benefit from creatine monohydrate. Published research studies have pointed to as high as 30% of athletes are non-responders and that they do not retain the creatine. I find it to be closer to 1 in 10 athletes and this is also situational, depending upon how intense their training plan is and what the creatine is stacked with. It may simply come down to creatine transport, and high glycemic carbohydrates like simple sugars may improve response for some athletes. I also find that when a select few athletes do not respond to a creatine load they likely do not respond to other anabolic agents either- kind of a curse for about 10% of all explosive athletes. Perhaps the non-responders need more creatine monohydrate, more amino acids, or other anabolic activators.

Also, taking creatine monohydrate can shut down the body's natural manufacture of creatine from amino acids. This is only natural because the body under a normal diet makes about 1-2 grams of creatine each day. Taking in 20 grams of powder creatine monohydrate as a load dose, or 5g as a maintenance dose, tells the body it no longer needs to make creatine- so it shuts this process down. A high red meat diet will do the same thing. When athletes cycle creatine, during the off-cycle the body again makes its own 1-2 grams of creatine.

Athletes and coaches often ask that if 5 grams is OK for a maintenance dose over weeks of use, would 10 grams a day long-term be any better? The answer is likely no in most cases. This is because the creatine stores become saturated, and any additional creatine is simply excreted- which the kidneys have to deal with.

One final question is whether or not athletes really need to cycle creatine. Some research has shown reduced efficiencies over time. I feel athletes should cycle creatine. I've never had a specific set period of use and period of break, but looking back over the past twenty years of using creatine monohydrate with many athletes I think it's good to cycle it. What type of cycling I'm not sure, but perhaps longer use cycles lasting 30 days during pre-season strength cycles followed by a five day washout would be appropriate. During in-season competition, perhaps a cycle of 20 days on coinciding with the most important competitions and 3-5 days off would be useful.

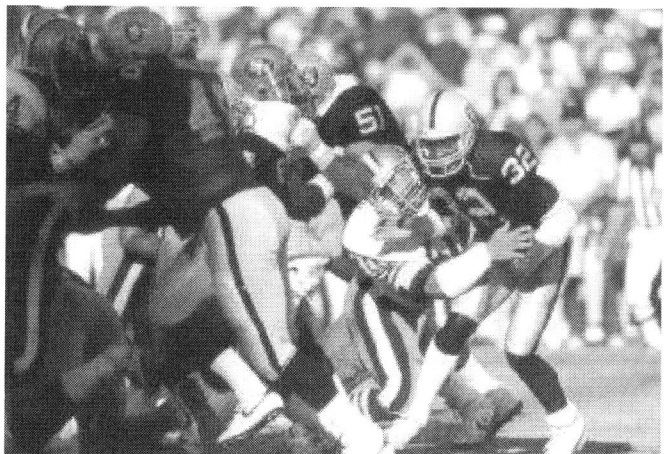
49er Riki Ellison putting a hit on Raider Marcus Allen. Brunner Photo.

TRI-METHYL GLYCINE (TMG, GLYCINE BETAINE)

Trimethylglycine (TMG) is an organic compound that occurs in plants. TMG was the first betaine discovered by researchers. Initially it was simply called betaine because it was discovered in sugar beets. Recent research lead to the discovery of many other betaines and so glycine betaine distinguishes this one. Today it is extracted from sugar beet molasses to yield a 99% pure material. TMG is often referred to as vitamin like because although humans can make it from choline, it can't be made in adequate quantities and needs to be included in the diet. Rich sources include the grain quinoa, spinach, wheat bran, and of course beets.

TMG is an important cofactor in methylation reactions, a process that occurs in every human cell to synthesize and donate methyl groups (CH3) for other processes in the body. These processes include the synthesis of neurotransmitters such as dopamine and serotonin. Methyl groups are also supplied to DNA which enhances gene expression.

I first learned about TMG in Leningrad Russia in 1989 and have been using it as an anabolic nutrient ever since, within various formulas. TMG was a favorite of the famous Soviet sport scientist Nikolai N. Yakovlev who is a pioneer of many sport biochemistry breakthroughs that sizably contributed to the success of Soviet sports as well as sport science worldwide. I know of no more influential researcher in sport biochemistry in the world.

In the 1950's Yakovlev discovered the phenomenon of supercompensation of muscle and liver glycogen and muscle phosphocreatine during training and in post-exercise recovery. From 1949 through 1976 he established the concept of the biochemical specificity of muscle cell response to different training methods, the biochemical restorative and adaptive capacity of exercised muscle, and the specificity of adaptation we utilize today. Sadly Nikolai did not enjoy retirement for long as he passed away in 1992 at a young 81 years of age.

Recognized in Russia and throughout the former East Bloc as a leading pioneer of modern exercise biochemistry, Yakovlev's lifetime work influenced research in many Soviet laboratories. He ended his prestigious career as the
Director of the Scientific Research Institute of Physical Culture in Leningrad (now St. Petersburg), Russia.

I'm excited to report that in just the past few years we've seen some sport specific research conducted in the west with TMG, especially at the University of Connecticut (Storrs) and the University of Memphis. This research further substantiates the findings conducted by Yakovlev and others decades ago.

Professor Nikolai N. Yakovlev (1911-1992). A founder of modern Soviet exercise biochemistry and former Director of the Research Institute of Physical Culture in Leningrad (St. Petersburg) Russia. Dr. Yakovlev was a pioneer in the research of nutritional ergogenics as they relate to the anabolic pathway in restoration and adaptation. Brunner Photo, 1989.

"Our aim was to examine the effect of betaine (B) supplementation on selected circulating hormonal measures and Akt muscle signaling proteins after an acute exercise session. Twelve trained men (age 19.7 ± 1.23 years) underwent 2 weeks of supplementation with either betaine (B) (1.25 g BID) or placebo (P). B increased resting Total muscle Akt ($p = 0.003$). B potentiated phosphorylation (relative to P) of Akt (Ser(473)) and p70 S6 k (Thr(389)) ($p = 0.016$ and $p = 0.005$, respectively). Phosphorylation of AMPK (Thr(172)) decreased during both treatments (both $p = 0.001$). Betaine (vs. placebo) supplementation enhanced both the anabolic endocrine profile and the corresponding anabolic signaling environment, suggesting increased protein synthesis."

Apicella JM, Lee EC, Bailey BL, Saenz C, Anderson JM, Craig SA, Kraemer WJ, Volek JS, Maresh CM. Betaine supplementation enhances anabolic endocrine and Akt signaling in response to acute bouts of exercise. Eur J Appl Physiol. 2013 Mar;113(3):793-802.

"Betaine (B) increased resting Total muscle Akt ($p = 0.003$). B potentiated phosphorylation (relative to P) of Akt (Ser(473)) and p70 S6 k (Thr(389)) ($p = 0.016$ and $p = 0.005$, respectively). Phosphorylation of AMPK (Thr(172)) decreased during both treatments (both $p = 0.001$). Betaine (vs. placebo) supplementation enhanced both the anabolic endocrine profile and the corresponding anabolic signaling environment, suggesting increased protein synthesis."

Apicella JM, Lee EC, Bailey BL, Saenz C, Anderson JM, Craig SA, Kraemer WJ, Volek JS, Maresh CM. Betaine supplementation enhances anabolic endocrine and Akt signaling in response to acute bouts of exercise. Eur J Appl Physiol. 2013 Mar;113(3):793-802.

"In conclusion, 15 days of betaine supplementation did not increase peak CON or ECC force outputs during an isokinetic chest press but did appear to reduce subjective measures of fatigue to the exercise protocol."

Hoffman JR, Ratamess NA, Kang J, Gonzalez AM, Beller NA, Craig SA. Effect of 15 days of betaine ingestion on concentric and eccentric force outputs during isokinetic exercise. J Strength Cond Res. 2011 Aug;25(8):2235-41.

"Our findings provide the first evidence that BET could promote muscle fibers differentiation and increase myotubes size by IGF-1 pathway activation, suggesting that BET might represent a possible new drug/integrator strategy, not only in sport performance but also in clinical conditions characterized by muscle function impairment."

Senesi P, Luzi L, Montesano A, Mazzocchi N, Terruzzi I. Betaine supplement enhances skeletal muscle differentiation in murine myoblasts via IGF-1 signaling activation. J Transl Med. 2013 Jul 19;11(1):174. Electronic published ahead of print.

In another useful study from Stuart Craig and others from the University of Connecticut (Storrs) their research showed that one week of oral TMG (1.25 grams twice daily) sizably improved cycling sprint power in recreationally active men and women athletes. Peak power increased by 3.4%, average mean power 3.3%, and maximum mean power 3.5% over the placebo.

Pryor JL, Craig SA, Swensen T. Effect of betaine supplementation on cycling sprint performance. J Int Soc Sports Nutr. 2012 Apr 3;9(1):12.

Stuart Craig, Richard Bloomer and team introduced the same 2.5 gram daily dose of TMG to men and found that "the betaine supplementation results in a moderate increase in total repetitions and volume load in the bench press exercise, without impacting other performance measures."

Trepanowski JF, Farney TM, McCarthy CG, Schilling BK, Craig SA, Bloomer RJ. The effects of chronic betaine supplementation on exercise performance, skeletal muscle oxygen saturation and associated biochemical parameters in resistance trained men. J Strength Cond Res. 2011 Dec;25(12):3461-71.

"The purpose of this study was to examine the efficacy of 15 days of betaine supplementation on muscle endurance, power performance and rate of fatigue in active college-aged men. CONCLUSION: Two-weeks of betaine supplementation in active, college males appeared to improve muscle endurance of the squat exercise, and increase the quality of repetitions performed."

Hoffman JR, Ratamess NA, Kang J, Rashti SL, Faigenbaum AD. Effect of betaine supplementation on power performance and fatigue. J Int Soc Sports Nutr. 2009 Feb 27;6:7.

TMG may be of functional use as both an anabolic ergogenic as well as having anti-inflammatory effects in older athletes, especially those having trouble keeping on muscle mass as well as increased inflammatory load. Earlier I mentioned that younger athletes must be careful when using any anti-inflammatory compounds including NSAIDs as certain cytokines like IL-6 are adaptive signaling molecules. With older athletes the inflammatory load may be sizably elevated beyond a hormetic zone of positive effect. TMG may help reduce excessive inflammation response by lowering NF-KB, COX-2, and TNF-α levels. This may do two things, reduce tissue damage, especially connective and joint tissue, and reduce anabolic resistance in muscles for better skeletal muscle synthesis.

Go EK, Jung KJ, Kim JM, Lim H, Lim HK, Yu BP, Chung HY. Betaine modulates age-related NF-kappaB by thiol-enhancing action. Biol Pharm Bull. 2007 Dec;30(12):2244-9.

My final thought about TMG (Betaine) is that, as an anabolic ergogenic, look for results over extended training programs. While the majority of human exercise research with TMG lasted only 15 days, in the real world I've found added benefits with extended use. Look for even larger anabolic influence in high-intensity resistance training cycles lasting 30 to 60 days. When combined with other useful nutritional ergogenics of anabolic focus TMG acts in synergy and is quite a powerful addition to influence muscle size, strength, and explosiveness. The daily dose I use is usually one gram divided into two 500mg doses up to three grams daily. Under most training situations I suggest you stick with a gram daily and increase up to threefold during short very intense cycles lasting a couple weeks where resistance training loads are very high.

"I think goals should never be easy, they should force you to work, even if they are uncomfortable at the time."
~ Michael Phelps

OMEGA-3 FATTY ACIDS

I know what you're thinking. Why would omega-3 fatty acids, specifically EPA and DHA from fish oil be on the anabolic list? At first glance it doesn't make sense. Let me explain why I've been recommending omega-3 oils to athletes for over twenty years.

Knowing that fatty acids are a major component of cell structure, be it a muscle cell or a nerve cell for example, it just makes sense that the ratio of various fatty acids is important to cell function and thus athletic performance. It's well accepted that the ratio of omega-6 fats to omega-3 fats are commonly imbalanced in the western diet and this leads to an increase in inflammation. Historically for thousands of years the ratio of O-6 to O-3 was most often 3:1 or 2:1. Today, due to the consumption of a lot of oils (i.e. corn, safflower, and sunflower) high in Omega-6, the ratio is often 15:1 and higher.

While both Omega-6 and Omega-3 are considered essential fatty acids, meaning our body cannot make them, the Omega-6 pathway is well recognized as being the more inflammatory pathway. Recall earlier that I discussed cytokines as signaling molecules for adaptation? Well, Omega-6 in excess ramps-up some pretty powerful inflammatory cytokines that in excess contribute to metabolic dysfunction. Omega imbalance is a key reason why older persons develop metabolic inflexibility leading to health conditions like Type-2 diabetes and obesity. When cells are clogged with the wrong ratio of fatty acids they become inflamed. When they become inflamed they spin off a lot of free radicals which further increases resistance and inflammation. This is called a closed loop and really one of the best ways to get out of the loop is to introduce more Omega-3 and consume less Omega-6 and less saturated fat like that found in corn fed beef, excessive use of butter, etc.

I'm convinced that a poor Omega-6 to Omega-3 ratio leads to anabolic resistance, more so in older master's athletes, but also in young athletes if their diet is not good. This resistance interferes with muscle growth and neuromuscular power.

Here's what Dr. Artemis Simopoulos, an international expert on essential fats and health has to say about Omega-6 and Omega-3:

"Today we live in a nutritional environment that is very different from the environments to which we are genetically adapted. Major changes in our food supply accompanied the domestication of animals and the agricultural revolution about 10,000 years ago. Later, the industrial revolution and developments in food technology brought about further major changes in the composition of foods, one of the most important of which was a change in the quantity and quality of the various fatty acids. The content of saturated fat and omega-6 essential fatty acids increased, whereas the content of omega-3 fatty acids decreased."

"It may therefore be very unfortunate that foods with a high ratio of linoleic acid (omega-6) to -linolenic acid (omega-3) of about 15/1, common in developed countries, are now spreading to developing countries adopting the agricultural and dietary practices of the so-called developed world. Studies of transgenic animals (the FAT-1 mouse) provided further support for the concept that the effects of high linoleic acid and arachidonic acid are detrimental and that the effects of α-linolenic acid, eicosapentaenoic acid and docosahexaenoic acid are beneficial."

"Decreasing omega-6 fatty acids and increasing omega-3 fatty acids in the diet, so that the ratio of omega-6 to omega-3 is reduced from typically 15: 1 or more to ideally 2: 1 or less is a nutritional policy that should be considered by national and international organizations, agricultural and health associations and food industry. It is consistent with results of basic research, current epidemiology and studies of evolution."

Simopoulos AP, Faergeman O, Bourne PG. Action plan for a healthy agriculture, healthy nutrition, healthy people. J Nutrigenet Nutrigenomics. 2011;4(2):65-8.

A very positive study was conducted by Gordon Smith, Michael Rennie and co-investigators in which they showed that Omega-3 combined with a strong insulin response and ample amino acids from the diet resulted in an increase in the anabolic response in both older and young men and women.

"We provide evidence that LCn-3PUFA supplementation causes a considerable increase in the muscle protein anabolic response to hyperinsulinemia-hyperaminoacidemia in healthy young and middle-aged adults. These data compliment and extend the results we recently obtained in older adults [9] and demonstrate that LCn-3PUFA supplementation not only alleviates the muscle protein anabolic resistance associated with old age [9, 30–32] but can actually boost the anabolic response to nutritional stimuli in healthy muscle from young and middle-aged adults."

"Our results indicate that LCn-3PUFA alone are not sufficient to elicit an anabolic effect (because the basal rate of muscle protein synthesis was not affected by LCn-3PUFA supplementation) but that they require additional anabolic stimuli such as amino acids and augment their anabolic effect by increasing the activation of the mTOR-p70s6k signaling pathway (which is considered an integral control point for muscle protein anabolism [33] and muscle cell growth [34–36]) and translational efficiency."

"Considering the observed changes in skeletal muscle phospholipid composition, it is also possible that LCn-3PUFA supplementation modulated key substrates along the anabolic signaling cascades by affecting membrane lipid composition and/or fluidity [39, 40]. For example, increased membrane DHA content activates PKC [39], which stimulates translational activity [41]. It is unlikely that the beneficial effect of LCn-3PUFA on muscle protein synthesis was related to their anti-inflammatory properties [42, 43] because our subjects were young and healthy and we did not detect any treatment-induced changes in inflammatory cytokine concentrations in plasma – most likely because the concentrations were very low to begin with."

Smith GI, Atherton P, Reeds DN, Mohammed BS, Rankin D, Rennie MJ, Mittendorfer B. Omega-3 polyunsaturated fatty acids augment the muscle protein anabolic response to hyperinsulinaemia-hyperaminoacidaemia in healthy young and middle-aged men and women. Clin Sci (Lond). 2011 Sep; 121(6):267-78.

Here are what two researchers from the University of Aberdeen in Scotland, Torkamol Kamolrat and Stuart Gray had to say about the anabolic effects of fish oil omega-3's:

"The aim of the current study was to determine the distinct effects of EPA and DHA on protein synthesis, protein breakdown and signaling pathways in C2C12 myotubes (author- A developing skeletal muscle fiber)."

"Data revealed that after incubation with EPA protein synthesis was 25% greater ($P<0.05$) compared to control cells, with no effect of DHA. Protein breakdown was 22% ($P<0.05$) lower, compared to control cells, after incubation with EPA, with no effect of DHA. Analysis of signalling pathways revealed that both EPA and DHA incubation increased ($P<0.05$) p70s6k phosphorylation, EPA increased ($P<0.05$) FOXO3a phosphorylation, with no alteration in other signalling proteins. The current study has demonstrated distinct effects of EPA and DHA on protein metabolism with EPA showing a greater ability to result in skeletal muscle protein accretion."

Kamolrat T, Gray SR. The effect of eicosapentaenoic and docosahexaenoic acid on protein synthesis and breakdown in murine C2C12 myotubes. Biochem Biophys Res Commun. 2013 Mar 22;432(4):593-8.

While I included Omega-3 EPA/DNA in this anabolic section of the book, it could just as easily go into the energetic or neurologic sections. In fact, this is originally why I recommended fish oil to athlete's years ago. I wanted them to be more explosive and more reactive and this has to do with both neuromuscular response as well as the ability to maintain explosive endurance. Two pertinent studies of omega-3 support its influence on neuromuscular response and reduced reaction time:

"Docosahexaenoic acid (DHA) is important for brain function, and its status is dependent on dietary intakes. Therefore, individuals who consume diets low in omega-3 (n-3) polyunsaturated fatty acids may cognitively benefit from DHA supplementation."

"Healthy adults (n = 176; age range: 18-45 y; nonsmoking and with a low intake of DHA) completed a 6-mo randomized, placebo-controlled, double-blind intervention in which they consumed 1.16 g DHA/d or a placebo."

"DHA supplementation improved memory and the reaction time (RT) of memory in healthy, young adults whose habitual diets were low in DHA."

Stonehouse W, Conlon CA, Podd J, Hill SR, Minihane AM, Haskell C, Kennedy D. DHA supplementation improved both memory and reaction time in healthy young adults: a randomized controlled trial. Am J Clin Nutr. 2013 May;97(5):1134-43.

An Italian study with Omega-3 and Policosanol (a natural mixture of long chain alcohols extracted from plant waxes, mostly from sugar cane and rice) showed the following:

"The purpose of this study was to determine the effect of omega-3 fatty acids and policosanol supplementation on the cognitive processes involved in the control of reactivity in karateka engaged in attention tests."

"Eighteen karateka were randomly assigned to 2 groups. One group (10 subjects) took the supplement of omega-3 fatty acids (2.25 g) plus policosanol (10 mg) (O3 + P) for 21 days, and the other group was supplemented with placebo (oleic sunflower oil)."

RESULTS:

"After 21 days of supplementation, subjects who received O3 + P showed a reduced reaction time and increased vigor sensation associated with a reduction of the negative states measured with the POMS test. Analysis of the event-related brain potentials showed a reduced latency of the movement-related brain macropotentials. In particular, the potentials recorded in the premotor period and motor period occurred earlier and the latency of EMG activation was reduced. In the third test, 21 days after the last O3 + P supplementation, the positive effects on the mood state persisted, while the reaction time, EMG, and brain potential latencies increased, although their values remained lower than in the first test. The placebo group did not show any significant differences in Tests 2 and 3 compared to Test 1 for either POMS or reactivity and brain potentials."

CONCLUSIONS:

"Supplementation with O3 + P may be effective in improving mood state and reactivity. The reaction time reduction appears to be due to a central nervous system effect, as shown by the reduced latency of movement-related brain macropotentials and EMG activation. These results are in line with previous experiments."

Fontani G, Lodi L, Migliorini S, Corradeschi F. Effect of omega-3 and policosanol supplementation on attention and reactivity in athletes. J Am Coll Nutr. 2009 Aug;28 Suppl:473S-481S.

Omega-3 EPA and DHA have been shown to increase skeletal muscle (especially Type I and IIa) blood flow. In just one dose blood flow can improve and in multi-doses over a couple of weeks the deformability (flexibility) of red blood cells (RBCs) improves as the Omega-3 fatty acids integrate into the cell wall of the RBC's. This helps boost oxygen carrying capacity and improve stamina and explosive endurance.

Omega-3 oils may have a positive influence on post-concussion restoration. Concussions are a complex pathophysiological process affecting the brain, induced by traumatic biomechanical forces. Currently the standard of care in the treatment for concussions is cognitive and physical rest until symptoms resolve with a graduated return to activity. High dose omega-3 fatty acids have shown to have anti-inflammatory, anti-oxidant, and membrane stabilizing properties. They have also been used in treatment of severe traumatic brain injury. Traumatic brain injury remains the most common cause of death in persons under 45 years of age in the Western world. Recent evidence from animal studies suggests that supplementation with omega-3 fatty acids (particularly eicosapentaenoic acid [EPA] and docosahexaenoic acid [DHA]) improves functional outcomes following neural injury. I feel Omega-3 is a viable nutrient for use in both the prevention and restoration from mild blunt head trauma as seen in sports.

Conclusion and Use of Omega-3

There are a lot of Omega-3 products on the market. I've focused on EPA and DHA which are downstream of the starting Omega-3 called alpha-linolenic acid or ALA. ALA is found in plant oils and seeds such as flax and chia. While many health food stores sell ground and whole flax and chia seeds plus their oil, I prefer the fish source of Omega-3 for athletic performance because it has EPA and DHA which have more "power" than ALA.

DHA can also be acquired from an algae source, so if an athlete is vegan they can always use the algae oil extract high in DHA along with flax and/or chia seeds, meal and oil. If you want to consume flax seeds they must be ground, as eating whole raw flax seeds can be dangerous as they do not digest well and can get caught in and inflame the intestines.

Whether you consume oils rich in ALA or EPA and DHA you should also limit your consumption of refined Omega-6 (linoleic acid) oils like corn oil, sunflower oil, grapeseed oil, cottonseed oil, walnut oil, soybean oil, and general vegetable oil which all have high ratios of the more inflammatory potentiating linoleic acid. The refined Omega-6 oils are often found in baked goods. It's not that Omega-6 fats are all bad. Omega-6 fats are essential to health. It's just that we generally get way too much of them which over-power any Omega-3 we consume. To get the ratio down to a healthy 2:1 or 6:3 (O-6/O-3) limit the Omega-6 oils and consume either a flax oil rich in ALA (1 Tablespoon has about 7.7 grams of total fats including 2.2g of Omega-3 and 2.5g of Omega-9) or some oil or oil filled softgels containing EPA and DHA. I prefer fish oil over cod liver oil as it generally has a better ratio and quantity of EPA and DHA.

You can mix and match your sources of Omega-3 oils such as using a flax oil and olive oil on salads or in a smoothie as well as a couple fish oil softgels daily. There are many fine fish oil softgels available. I prefer fish oil in the triglyceride form which is the form naturally found in fish. When fish oil is distilled (cooked at very high temperature) the triglyceride backbone of the molecule separates and the oil becomes an ethyl-ester form. The ethyl-ester form still performs well, but the triglyceride form has some good scientific support showing 30% faster absorption.

In addition to traditional fish oils, there are new patented technologies available called Vesisorb® (Vesifact, Baar, Switzerland) where the fish oil is emulsified (made water friendly) and disperses in micro-sized particles (colloidal technology) for super-efficient absorption, upwards of 5 times better absorption than ordinary Omega-3 fish oil. This is a very economical way to get fish oil and you only need 1-2 softgels a day versus 5 to 10 of older technologies. Two softgels using Vesisorb® technology supplies 330mg of EPA and 220mg DHA (550mg total Omega-3) with enhanced absorption- this is all you need. If you use ordinary fish oil consume between 2,000 and 3,000 mg's daily in divided doses.

Do not fear fats. The right fats can be very healthy and help enhance athletic performance, helping your muscle cells and nerve cells react faster and with more power. Limit your consumption of fatty foods that generally have way too much highly processed saturated fats and Omega-6 fats. Unlike all the health books which promote a vegan diet and no animal products, I recommend some animal fats from grass fed animal meats if possible (more expensive than pen-fed animals) but worth it in quality, as well as eggs and milk. Consume some butter also as it contains cholesterol which is needed for testosterone production. I use stick butter or butter mixed with olive oil (rich in omega-9). Read the label as many blended butter products contain a lot of added junk. The one I use is by Land O Lakes® and just has butter olive oil and salt added.

"I've worked too hard and too long to let anything stand in the way of my goals. I will not let my teammates down and I will not let myself down."
~ Mia Hamm

PHOSPHATIDIC ACID

How does resistance exercise promote muscle growth? This has been the subject of intense research for many years. Much of the new research has shown that resistance exercise promotes skeletal muscle growth via the mammalian target of rapamycin (mTORC1) pathway. No active mTORC1, no muscle growth!

The cellular mechanism(s) linked to stimulating mTORC1 signaling after muscle contraction has been the subject of new research which shows that several roads lead to the activation of mTORC1. And as an athlete you should leverage all of these anabolic roads to maximize gains in muscle mass, strength, power, and explosiveness.

Muscle contractions during resistance exercise are one such road. This road makes phosphatidic acid (PA) from phosphatidylcholine (PCh) via the enzyme Phospholipase D (PLD) which is located in the plasma membrane of the muscle cell. PA is a phospholipid that makes up a small percentage of the phospholipid pool and is part of all cell membranes. It is extremely short lived and is rapidly hydrolysed by the enzyme PA phosphohydrolase to form diacylglycerol (DAG). PA is an anabolic trigger for mTORC1.

Muscle Contractions → PLD→ PCh→ PA→ mTORC1 → P70S6 Kinase→ Muscle Growth

A landmark study on the role of muscle contraction, PA, and mTOR was published in 2009 by Troy Hornberger and team from the University of Wisconsin. They discovered that muscle contractions activate mTORC1 through a pathway independent of other anabolic pathways that activate mTORC1. This pathway produces PA to boost mTORC1.

O'Neil TK, Duffy LR, Frey JW, Hornberger TA. The role of phosphoinositide 3-kinase and phosphatidic acid in the regulation of mammalian target of rapamycin following eccentric contractions. J Physiol. 2009 Jul 15;587(Pt 14):3691-701.

Resent research suggests that the ingestion of PA in combination with resistance training stimulates greater gains in muscle strength and mass than resistance training alone. A recent proof-of-concept study by Jay Hoffman, Jeff Stout and research team found great potential for PA in strength training cycles. Five capsules containing 150mg of PA each (750 milligrams per day) were consumed daily (no set time of use) by weight training subjects. All subjects using PA or placebo trained 4 times each week for 8 weeks with loads of 10-12 reps of 1-RM. Subjects who consumed PA showed a 12.7% increase in squat strength while placebo showed a 9.3% increase. A 1-RM for the bench press showed a gain of 5.1% in PA users and 3.3% in placebo users. PA users showed a 3.5 pound increase in muscle mass while the placebo group showed a small quarter pound increase.

Hoffman JR, Stout JR, Williams DR, Wells AJ, Fragala MS, Mangine GT, Gonzalez AM, Emerson NS, McCormack WP, Scanlon TC, Purpura M, Jäger R. Efficacy of phosphatidic acid ingestion on lean body mass, muscle thickness and strength gains in resistance-trained men. J Int Soc Sports Nutr. 2012 Oct 5;9(1):47.

Take Away: Signaling by mTORC1 is a well-recognized component of the pathway through which mechanical signals regulate protein synthesis and muscle mass. PA Induces mTORC1 signaling via an ERK-independent mechanism. PA should be an excellent addition to any resistance training program, especially when muscle contractions are really intense and the goal is an increase in muscle mass, strength, and explosiveness. Since it's a short lived substance it may be good to consume a couple hundred milligrams per dose a few times each day. PA may further help amplify the mTORC1 pathway's anabolic action when combined with other anabolic ergogenic compounds including whey proteins, l-leucine and HMB, and creatine monohydrate.

You will only find PA in the branded product Mediator® which was researched and developed by Chemi Nutra, the US entity of Chemi S.p.A., a privately held pharmaceutical and nutraceutical company based in Milan, Italy. I've always appreciated Chemi Nutra nutritionals because of their quality and science based rationale. Mediator® is a great addition to Chemi Nutra's athletic performance enhancement nutrient AlphaSize® α-GPC for neuromuscular explosiveness.

While more research will no doubt be conducted using Mediator® to support athletic performance and anabolism, as well as to maintain muscle mass and strength in aging individuals, a good starting point for oral use is around 700 milligrams of

PA daily. This was shown in a research paper I cited previously. I do not see Mediator® being a pre-workout supplement because muscle contraction itself stimulates PA production. After-exercise and several hours later it should be a strong trigger to maintain mTORC1 in exercise recovery and extended adaptation.

"I played football for a team called the East Dragons on the east side of town. We only had six regular season games. And in six games I played tail back and I had 18 touchdowns. That's when I knew I had some athletic ability."
~ LeBron James

MINERAL OROTATES

I first learned about mineral orotates when I was traveling in Bulgaria and Russia in 1988. I had never heard of them before but the team physicians and coaches spoke highly of them and were giving them to their elite athletes. I began using orotates in various formulas back in 1990, with good results. I continue to recommend them because they are quite anabolic.

Minerals like calcium, magnesium and potassium are bound (chelated) to orotic acid (OA) to form a mineral orotate. For many years it was believed to be part of the Vitamin B complex and was called vitamin B13, but it is now known that it is not a vitamin. One of the main advantages of mineral orotates is their ability to be easily absorbed through the digestive tract and to penetrate the outer and inner layers of cells. Calcium, magnesium and potassium are all very important in muscle contractions and growth. Magnesium and potassium are essential for enzyme activity including the mTORC1 pathway. Mineral orotates function as a very efficient carrier of the mineral portion into muscle cells.

There are two parts to any mineral complex: The mineral such as calcium (Ca), magnesium (Mg), potassium (K), or zinc (Zn) and what the mineral is bound to. For example, magnesium bound to citric acid (an acid found in fruits) is called magnesium citrate, while potassium bound to aspartic acid is known as potassium aspartate.

Hans Nieper was a well know orthomolecular physician who often recommended mineral orotates because of their efficient targeted delivery to cells. He often used these mineral orotates as efficient transporters to deliver the minerals to specific target tissues.

While the mineral portion of mineral orotates is important in cell health in its own right, another major reason why Soviet athletes were given mineral orotates was because of the orotic acid itself. OA is a key intermediate in making pyrimidines and purines and is shown to stimulate the synthesis of glycogen and ATP which stimulates the energy status of muscle and nerve cells. Because binding sites for Mg(ATP) are provided by OA it is often classified as a Mg-fixing agent. Pyrimidine nucleotides are important constituents of phospholipids (structural components) in cell membranes such as the sarcolemma of muscle tissue. These nucleotides are also important constituents of RNA, the building blocks of new muscle and other cellular tissues. Boosting the synthesis of RNA's is perhaps the greatest benefit of OA in muscle protein synthesis.

Magnesium orotate maintains muscle cell efficiency during intense repetitive contractions to improve exercise tolerance. It also has a positive influence on heart and blood vessel health and improves the utilization of fatty acids, activity of lipoprotein lipase, expression of genes of peroxisome proliferator-activated receptor alpha (PPARα) and its target enzymes. This helps cells utilize fatty acids as fuels.

"In conclusion, PPARalpha intron 7 G/C polymorphism was associated with physical performance in Russian athletes, and this may be explained, in part, by the association between PPARalpha genotype and muscle fiber type composition."

Ahmetov II, Mozhayskaya IA, Flavell DM, Astratenkova IV, Komkova AI, Lyubaeva EV, Tarakin PP, Shenkman BS, Vdovina AB, Netreba AI, Popov DV, Vinogradova OL, Montgomery HE, Rogozkin VA. PPARalpha gene variation and physical performance in Russian athletes. Eur J Appl Physiol. 2006 May;97(1):103-8.

Geiss KR, Stergiou N, Jester, Neuenfeld HU, Jester HG. Effects of magnesium orotate on exercise tolerance in patients with coronary heart disease. Cardiovasc Drugs Ther. 1998 Sep;12 Suppl 2:153-6.

Traut TW, Jones ME. Uracil metabolism--UMP synthesis from orotic acid or uridine and conversion of uracil to beta-alanine: enzymes and cDNAs. Prog Nucleic Acid Res Mol Biol. 1996;53:1-78.

"Chronic administration of potassium orotate to rats per os in doses of 5, 10, 20, 50 and 100 mg/kg was followed by different correlations of the training under stress with anxiolytic activity. The doses of the drug were defined, at which the maximally pronounced effects under consideration were in optimal correlations, as were doses which entailed inhibition of the training in the presence of a relatively low tranquilizing activity, low emotional responsiveness and aggressiveness. It is suggested that natural analogs of pyrimidine, whose precursor is orotic acid, are universal endogenous regulators of mnemonic and antianxiety functions."

Karkishchenko NN, Khaïtin MI. [Quantitative evaluation of the anxiolytic and nootropic effects of potassium orotate in a wide range of doses]. Farmakol Toksikol. 1986 Jan-Feb;49(1):14-6.

Below is a German study showing the use of magnesium to improve muscle sensitivity to insulin. Mg Orotate would be a very functional nutrient to maintain high insulin sensitivity which is important for insulin and IGF-1 use as well as turning on the mTORC1 pathway:

"Mg supplementation resulted in a significant improvement of fasting plasma glucose and some insulin sensitivity indices (ISIs) compared to placebo. Blood pressure and lipid profile did not show significant changes. The results provide significant evidence that oral Mg supplementation improves insulin sensitivity even in normomagnesemic, overweight, non-diabetic subjects emphasizing the need for an early optimization of Mg status to prevent insulin resistance and subsequently type 2 diabetes."

Mooren FC, Krüger K, Völker K, Golf SW, Wadepuhl M, Kraus A. Oral magnesium supplementation reduces insulin resistance in non-diabetic subjects - a double-blind, placebo-controlled, randomized trial. Diabetes Obes Metab. 2011 Mar;13(3):281-4.

Is muscle resistance to insulin prevalent in young athletes? The answer is likely no, but as an athlete gains experience and begins training at a very high level of volume and intensity it is not uncommon to have disruption of the handling of insulin and the maintenance of cell energetics. The strenuous energy-demanding work of both overreaching and overtraining can create a metabolic stress-like condition including signs of insulin resistance and deteriorated intracellular glucose availability. This can lead to the compromised fuelling of ion pumps which can result in a disturbed cellular osmoregulation indicated by taurine efflux and cellular swelling. Mg Orotate can help prevent this during high intensity high volume exercise to maintain good cell energetics, anabolic activity, and sport result.

Here is the summary from another German study where triathletes consumed Mg Orotate for four weeks and then competed in a short triathlon:

"In a double-blind randomized study, 23 competitive triathletes competing in an event consisting of a 500-meter swim, a 20-km bicycle race, and a 5-km run were studied after 4-week supplementation with placebo or 17 mmol/d Mg orotate. The tests were carried out without a break. Blood was collected before and after the test, and between the different events for assaying energy stress and membrane metabolism. Swimming, cycling, and running times decreased in the Mg-orotate group compared with the controls. Serum glucose concentration increased 87% during the test in the control group and 118% in the Mg-orotate group, while serum insulin increased 39% in the controls and decreased 65% in the Mg-orotate group. Venous O2 partial pressure increased 126% during the test in the controls and increased 208% in the Mg-orotate group. Venous CO2 partial pressure after the bicycle race decreased 66% (significantly) in the Mg-orotate group compared with 74% in the controls. Blood proton concentration decreased to 90% in the Mg-orotate group (significantly) compared with 98% in the controls. Blood leukocyte count increased from 5.92/nL to 11.0/nL in the controls and from 5.81/nL to 9.10/nL in the Mg-orotate group, a significant difference. Serum cortisol was lower in the Mg-orotate group before and after the test compared with the controls. CK catalytic concentration after the test was elevated 140% in the controls compared with 122% Mg-orotate group. The stress-induced modifications of energy and hormone metabolism described in this study indicate altered glucose utilization after Mg-Orotate supplementation and a reduced stress response without affecting competitive potential."

Golf SW, Bender S, Grüttner J. On the significance of magnesium in extreme physical stress. Cardiovasc Drugs Ther. 1998 Sep; 12 Suppl 2:197-202.

Orotic Acid →UMP→RNA and DNA Synthesis →Enhanced Muscle Growth

Most research has shown that administration of orotic acid leads to a greater production of nucleic acid precursors and concentrations of various pyrimidine cofactors essential for the metabolism of fats, carbohydrates, and proteins. The overall effect would be to promote growth and increase the pathways where pyrimidine cofactors function.

I've recommended mineral orotates for the past twenty years and have seen excellent results in their ability to support gains in muscle size, strength, and explosiveness. I mainly use magnesium and potassium orotates but calcium orotate is OK as well, and may be quite useful in maintaining intracellular Ca^{2+} for powerful muscle contractions. Mineral orotates include the elemental part (the mineral) and the orotic acid. They are reacted and as such are a new molecule. They do not disassociate in the gut like other mineral chelates which is why they are efficient at reaching target cells where the mineral can be delivered and the orotic acid can have its influence on cell energetics and anabolism.

Calcium orotate is about 11% elemental calcium, the rest being orotic acid. Magnesium orotate is 7% elemental and potassium orotate is about 20% elemental. Athletes can consume up to 3,000 milligrams (3 grams) of mineral orotates daily in divided doses of 1,000 mg during ultra-high intensity training cycles lasting 15-30 days, while daily mineral orotate doses of 1,000 mg should be used during lower intensity and tapering/restorative cycles. Mineral orotates can be used with other mineral chelates such as Mg and K succinates and Mg and K aspartates for great effect. I often use calcium, magnesium and potassium in the form of Ca citrate, aspartate, succinate, and malate. If calcium itself is the major focus for bone health, and not what it is chelated to, hydroxyapatite or carbonate forms work well.

In regard to potassium in the diet, its influence on health and athletic performance is underappreciated. You may have heard of the Paleolithic (Paleo) diet which has become a new diet craze. Our early ancestors consumed a diet very different from the modern diet we see today. With all the "organic" and "non-GMO" marketing hype surrounding food sales today, much of that is directed toward snack foods which really are little more than glorified junk foods.

The diet of our ancestors over hundreds of thousands of years of evolution consisted of organic, raw fruits and vegetables, seeds, and nuts, and wild grass fed animal meats. Simply eating organically grown fruits and vegetables is a solid start to maintain health and boost athletic performance. One mineral rich in organic vegetables and fruits is potassium. Potassium is the main intracellular cation which contributes to keeping the intracellular membrane potential slightly negative and elicits contraction of smooth, skeletal and cardiac muscle. A change in potassium intake modifies both cardiovascular and renal tubular function. If you want powerful muscle contractions you need a certain amount of potassium in your diet.

But diets today are often very low in potassium. Compared with the Stone Age Paleo diet, the modern human diet is both excessive in salt (NaCl) and deficient in fruits and vegetables which are rich in K^+ and bicarbonate (HCO_3)- -yielding organates like citrate. With the modern diet, the K^+/Na^+ ratio and the HCO_3^-/Cl^- ratio have both become reversed. Yet, the biologic machinery that evolved to process these dietary electrolytes remains largely unchanged, genetically fixed in Paleolithic times. Thus, the electrolytic mix of the modern diet is greatly mismatched to cellular processing machinery, especially in explosive trained athletes.

The daily needs of potassium for an athlete are between 3,500mg and 5,000mg. From my observations of many athletic diets, the vast majority of athletes consume far less than this, often one gram or less per day. Foods highest in potassium include white beans (1,000mg in one cup of cooked beans), dark greens like spinach (800mg in 1 cup cooked), baked potatoes with skin (900mg in an average sized spud), dried apricots (750mg in ½ cup), baked acorn squash (900mg in 1 cup cubed), plain yogurt (625mg in 1 cup), salmon (500mg in 3 ounces of fish), avocados (975mg in average size), mushrooms (430mg in one cup), coconut water (450mg in 8 ounces) and bananas (400mg in an average size banana). Eating more plant strong foods will sizably raise potassium, magnesium, and calcium consumption which will help with performance and restoration. Supplemental sources of potassium from potassium orotate, aspartate, and other chelates will help as well, but should be secondary to a good base diet. I recommend a potassium to sodium ratio (K/Na) of well above 2 and preferably 5 (5,000mg K and 1,000mg Na).

TAURINE

I have not used the amino acid taurine, but reviewing the thousands of journal articles in preparation of this book I came upon some interesting research on taurine, mainly on endurance performance but also anabolic activity that is promising. Taurine is a semi-essential non-protein sulfur containing amino acid that is abundant in skeletal muscle. That's important because sulfur itself is needed in a bunch of metabolic reactions, not the least of which is connective tissue health. It is the most abundant free amino acid in the heart, skeletal muscle, retina (containing rods and cones in the eye for sight and reaction time), and leukocytes (white blood cells as part of the immune system).

Taurine has both long-term and short-term actions in muscle. Short-term taurine modulates ion channel gating and calcium handling in muscle contractions. Long-term it has a positive influence on protein translation via AKT/mTORC1.

Taurine has been shown to improve the amount of phosphatidylcholine (PC) which is important in cell membrane structure, fluidity, and activity of muscle membrane enzymes and transporters. This can have a positive influence on muscle contractions such as force output-important to explosive athletes. Taurine is also shown to modulate oxidative stress and twitch rate of fast-twitch muscle fibers during prolonged stimulation during exercise.

In endurance exercise taurine is shown to reduce exercise-induced muscle fatigue, reduce lactate concentration (perhaps using it as fuel via the lactate shuttle), and increase the use of fats during muscle contraction. This may be of benefit during repetitive explosive movements during competition such as in team sports like football, hockey, basketball, lacrosse, soccer, and rugby, as well as in events like Nordic skiing and rowing.

"Moreover, inhibition of cellular taurine uptake by β-alanine and taurine transporter knockdown promoted taurine-induced cell proliferation, ERK and Akt activation, and in vivo angiogenesis, suggesting that extracellular taurine induces angiogenesis. However, taurine did not induce vascular inflammation and permeability in vitro and in vivo. These data demonstrate that extracellular taurine promotes angiogenesis by Akt- and ERK-dependent cell cycle progression and Src/FAK-mediated cell migration without inducing vascular inflammation, indicating that it is potential use for the treatment of vascular dysfunction-associated human diseases."

Baek YY, Cho DH, Choe J, Lee H, Jeoung D, Ha KS, Won MH, Kwon YG, Kim YM. Extracellular taurine induces angiogenesis by activating ERK-, Akt-, and FAK-dependent signal pathways. Eur J Pharmacol. 2012 Jan 15;674(2-3):188-99.

Activation of the Akt/mTORC1 pathway and its downstream targets, p70S6K and PHAS-1/4E-BP1, is active in regulating skeletal muscle fiber size.

Bodine SC, Stitt TN, Gonzalez M, Kline WO, Stover GL, Bauerlein R, Zlotchenko E, Scrimgeour A, Lawrence JC, Glass DJ, Yancopoulos GD. Akt/mTOR pathway is a crucial regulator of skeletal muscle hypertrophy and can prevent muscle atrophy in vivo. Nat Cell Biol. 2001 Nov;3(11):1014-9

The mechanism of taurine-induced heart and skeletal muscle protection involves activation of specific survival signals and anabolic PI3-K/Akt pathway as well as the inhibition of p53, JNK, p38 and NFκB catabolic pathways.

Taurine → IGF-1→ PI3K →AKT →mTORC1 →p70S6K and 4E-BP→Skeletal muscle growth

The dosage used in most research studies with men and women subjects is 1,500 mg prior to exercise or in daily use.

Additional Taurine Research:

Schuller-Levis GB, Park E. Taurine and its chloramine: modulators of immunity. Neurochem Res. 2004 Jan;29(1):117-26.

Imagawa TF, Hirano I, Utsuki K, Horie M, Naka A, Matsumoto K, Imagawa S. Caffeine and taurine enhance endurance performance. Int J Sports Med. 2009 Jul;30(7):485-8.

Goodman CA, Horvath D, Stathis C, Mori T, Croft K, Murphy RM, Hayes A. Taurine supplementation increases skeletal muscle force production and protects muscle function during and after high-frequency in vitro stimulation. J Appl Physiol (1985). 2009 Jul;107(1):144-54.

Rutherford JA, Spriet LL, Stellingwerff T. The effect of acute taurine ingestion on endurance performance and metabolism in well-trained cyclists. Int J Sport Nutr Exerc Metab. 2010 Aug;20(4):322-9.

Schaffer SW, Jong CJ, Ramila KC, Azuma J. Physiological roles of taurine in heart and muscle. J Biomed Sci. 2010 Aug 24;17 Suppl 1:S2.

Balshaw TG, Bampouras TM, Barry TJ, Sparks SA. The effect of acute taurine ingestion on 3-km running performance in trained middle-distance runners. Amino Acids. 2013 Feb;44(2):555-61.

Miyazaki T, Honda A, Ikegami T, Matsuzaki Y. The role of taurine on skeletal muscle cell differentiation. Adv Exp Med Biol. 2013;776:321-8.

"At the end of the day, we're trying to be the very best we can be and if we go out every day with that intent, I think we'll be alright."
~ Patrick Willis

PLANT BASED ECDYSTERONES

During my travels throughout the Soviet Union in the late 80's and early 90's I learned about a steroid from plants called 20-hydroxyecdysterone (20-Ecd) that since the 1970's was shown to have anabolic activity in animals and man. I purchased material from the research facility in Tashkent, Uzbekistan and supplied athletes worldwide with 5mg dose tablets. Later, as demand rose, we sourced 20-Ecd from specific Pfaffia paniculata root stocks from Brazil. The product name was Retibol® and the ingredient name was Ekdisten®.

The ecdysteroid 20-Ecd was first identified in plants during the mid-1960's. Rhaponticum carthamoides, also known as Leuzea carthamoides, possesses the highest level of ecdysteroids in newly developed shoots in the spring during rapid growth via transfer from the roots. Ajuga (i.e. turkistanica and remota) and Serratula (coronata) plants tend to have a higher amount of 20-Ecd in aerial parts such as leaves.

Phytoecdysteroids are the plant analogues of insect growth hormones. In insects, 20-hydroxyecdysone regulates the molting cycle (insects shed one form for another). Plants make 20-hydroxyecdysone to prevent insects from doing damage. The insect chews on the plant, ingests some 20-Ecd, and morphs (from larvae) into a flying insect (adult) and moves on, leaving the plant alone. Plants like spinach which have high levels of 20-Ecd have few pests that eat its leaves.

Adler JH, Grebenok RJ. Biosynthesis and distribution of insect-molting hormones in plants--a review. Lipids. 1995 Mar;30(3):257-62.

One of the primary researchers into the effects of 20-Ecd on humans is Dr. Vladimir Syrov. He was the first to establish that 20-Ecd stimulates the activity of ribosomes in protein translation. Later this translation process was further refined to reveal the influence of the PI3K/AKT and mTORC1 pathway. This is just what we like to see in a nutritional ergogenic with anabolic activity.

While Vladimir Syrov was conducting his research in Taskent, Uzbekistan, another 20-Ecd researcher in Kiev in the Ukraine, Dr. Julie Kholodova was also investigating the anabolic and restorative effects of this phytosteroid. Both Drs. Syrov and Kholodova answered many of my questions about the potential of 20-Ecd in human nutrition. In a letter to me, Dr. Syrov writes:

"According to the decision of the Pharmacologic Committee of the Ministry of Health in the USSR, ecdysten was on trial at various medical institutions. Clinical trials at 7 clinics in Moscow, Kiev, and Leningrad has shown that ecdysten considerably improves general state, increases general tonus, reinforces capacity for work, raises body muscle mass in lowered nutrition as a result of disorders in protein synthesis of various etiology. Thus, ecdysten normalizes body's mass, exerts a positive influence on metabolic figures of cardiac muscle."

"Ecdysten exerts more pronounced tonic effect than saparal (a popular adaptogenic supplement in the USSR) in somatic patients and especially in sportsmen during intensive training loads. 89% of 112 sportsmen noticed sooner disappearance of tiredness, apathy, improvement in endurance of loads in sports such as track and field athletics (jumps and running at medium distance), swimming, figure skating, high-speed skating, and ski racing."

"The most important advantage of ecdysten to saparal is its capacity to exert anabolic effects besides tonic action. Anabolic effect of ecdysten was confirmed by clinical and laboratory investigations (increase of body's mass, hemoglobin and erythrocyte content, increase of total serum protein, decrease of urea level, data of body composition, etc.)."

"The clinical trials of ecdysten permit us to conclude: (1) It is recommended to use as agent of general tonic action with simultaneous anabolic effect; (2) Ecdysten is effective also in medical and biological correction of sports activity, especially in the cases of the necessity to improve high-speed and power qualities and increase the functional state of muscular system. Use of ecdysten by sportsmen doesn't contradict the requirements of doping control; and (3) Unlike steroid anabolic preparations (methylandrostendiol, nerobol, nerobolil, etc.), ecdysten exerting anabolic influence doesn't manifest hormonal effects (first of all androgenic) and may be recommended in the cases when prescription of steranabols is undesirable."

Personal letter from V.N. Syrov, 1994

"In experiments with white mice it has been established that phytoecdisteroides turkesteron, ecdisteron and 2-desoxy-alpha-ecdison in the dose of 5 mg on 1 kg of body mass stimulate the protein synthesis. Using the model of protein synthesis from mice liver it has been shown that the action of phytoecdisteroides is connected with the rise of poliribosome functional activity and rate increase of protein macromolecules formation."

"It has been concluded that the anabolic effect of phytoecdisteroides in mammals organism is connected not with induction of RNA synthesis but with the acceleration of translocation processes."

Syrov VN. Mechanism of the anabolic action of phytoecdisteroids in mammals. Nauchnye Doki Vyss Shkoly Biol Nauki. 1984;(11):16-20.

"The results of the comparative study on the myotropic activity of methandrostenolone and ecdysterone and their effects on physical endurance of animals suggested that ecdysterone possessing a wider spectrum of the anabolic action on the contractile proteins of the skeletal muscles exerts a more pronounced influence on physical endurance of animals without their preliminary training."

Chermnykh NS, Shimanovskiĭ NL, Shutko GV, Syrov VN. The action of methandrostenolone and ecdysterone on the physical endurance of animals and on protein metabolism in the skeletal muscles. Farmakol Toksikol. 1988 Nov-Dec;51(6):57-60.

The Raskin laboratory at Rutgers University in New Jersey has conducted extensive investigation into the mechanism of anabolic action of ecdysterones. In their opinion the cellular mode of action involves calcium ion activity. Calcium ions function as signaling molecules in many cell processes.

Calcium ions (Ca2+) play a pivotal role in the physiology and biochemistry of organisms and the cell. It plays an important role in signal transduction pathways, where it acts as a second messenger, in neurotransmitter release from neurons and contraction of all muscle cell types. Many enzymes require calcium ions as a cofactor. Ilya Raskin discovered that 20-Ecd stimulates a rise in intracellular Ca(2+) which triggers mTORC1 via the PI3K/AKT pathway. One major result of interest to athletes is a rise in skeletal muscle protein translation resulting in muscle cell growth (for new muscle, recovery from exercise or competition, and when increasing explosive power) and metabolism.

"Phytoecdysteroids, structurally similar to insect molting hormones, produce a range of effects in mammals, including increasing growth and physical performance. In skeletal muscle cells, phytoecdysteroids increase protein synthesis. In this study we show that in a mouse skeletal muscle cell line, C(2)C(12), 20-hydroxyecdysone (20HE), a common phytoecdysteroid in both insects and plants, elicited a rapid elevation in intracellular calcium, followed by sustained Akt activation and increased protein synthesis. The effect was inhibited by a G-protein coupled receptor (GPCR) inhibitor, a phospholipase C (PLC) inhibitor, and a phosphoinositide kinase-3 (PI3K) inhibitor."

Gorelick-Feldman J, Cohick W, Raskin I. Ecdysteroids elicit a rapid Ca2+ flux leading to Akt activation and increased protein synthesis in skeletal muscle cells. Steroids. 2010 Oct;75(10):632-7.

"20-Hydroxyecdysone (20E) is an ecdysteroid hormone that regulates moulting in insects. Interestingly, 20E is also found most abundantly in plant species and has anabolic effects in vertebrates, i.e. increasing muscle size without androgen influence. The effect of 20E on slow and fast fiber types of skeletal muscle has not been reported yet. Here we present that 20E affects the size (cross-sectional area, CSA) of the different fiber types in a muscle-specific manner. The effect on fiber size was modified by the distance from the site of the treatment and the presence of a regenerating soleus muscle in the animal. Besides the fiber size, 20E also increased the myonuclear number in the fibers of normal and regenerating muscles, suggesting the activation of satellite cells. According to our results 20E may provide an alternative for substitution of anabolic-androgenic steroids in therapeutic treatments against muscle atrophy."

Tóth N, Szabó A, Kacsala P, Héger J, Zádor E. 20-Hydroxyecdysone increases fiber size in a muscle-specific fashion in rat. Phytomedicine. 2008 Sep;15(9):691-8

Below is a summary of a study conducted by Richard Kreider and his team where they gave strength athletes three different compounds, one being 20-Ecd, and put them through an eight week training cycle. The study was not positive for 20-Ecd.

I would like to address this study specifically because, while it was a valid test on strength-trained athletes, and the Kreider lab is an excellent research group, the lack of positive results from 20-Ecd is explainable: (1) I have never used even close to the dosage of 20-Ecd in this study. A dose of 200mg of 20-Ecd is a slug of plant steroids. In Russia the recommended dose for humans is 10mg twice daily and for athletes up to 50mg/day maximum. Mice studies have all used a dose 5-10mg/kg and have shown good anabolic effects. The human equivalent of this is 25-50mg's.

Giving a dose eight times the standard dose, which follows a "more is better" philosophy, is treading on shaky ground. 20-Ecd is a hormetin, meaning it is beneficial in a low dose but toxic in a high dose. Remember, 20-Ecd is made by plants as a natural insecticide. It is a potential toxin and as such, more is not always better. In fact it can be worse that not taking it at all when consumed in high amounts.

(2) 20-Ecd functions within a non-hormonal anabolic milieu (environment), not as a stand-alone. I've never recommended it be used by itself because from experience it likely will not produce optimal results. Yet add some other anabolic ergogenic nutrients such as whey protein, creatine, and mineral orotates to the mix along with higher load training and the influence on recovery and adaptive response is solid.

"Anabolic/catabolic analysis revealed no significant differences among groups in active testosterone (AT), free testosterone (FT), cortisol, the AT to cortisol ratio, urea nitrogen, creatinine, the blood urea nitrogen to creatinine ratio."

"Forty-five resistance-trained males (20.5 +/- 3 yrs; 179 +/- 7 cm, 84 +/- 16 kg, 17.3 +/- 9% body fat) were matched according to FFM and randomly assigned to ingest in a double blind manner supplements containing either a placebo (P); 800 mg/day of M; 200 mg of E; or, 1,000 mg/day of CSP3 for 8-weeks during training."

"Results indicate that M, E, and CSP3 supplementation do not affect body composition or training adaptations nor do they influence the anabolic/catabolic hormone status or general markers of catabolism in resistance-trained males."

Wilborn CD, Taylor LW, Campbell BI, Kerksick C, Rasmussen CJ, Greenwood M, Kreider RB. Effects of methoxyisoflavone, ecdysterone, and sulfo-polysaccharide supplementation on training adaptations in resistance-trained males. J Int Soc Sports Nutr. 2006 Dec 13;3:19-27.

"Serratula coronata and Serratula inermis (fam. Asteraceae) have been chosen as the most perspective sources for ecdysteroids from the flora of Ukraine. Ecdysterone was the major component in both species (approximately 2%). Antioxidant activity, antiradical and immunomodulators effects, anabolic, adaptogenic, stimulating, hypocholesterolemic, hepatoprotective actions have been found on the variety of model systems in vitro and in vivo (D-hypovitaminosis, hypercholesterolemia, liver intoxication, increased physical loading). A number of preparations-biostumulators have been elaborated on the basis of ecdysteroids from Serratula sp.--for poultry-keeping, agricultural entomology and as food supplements
for sick or healthy people."

Kholodova Y. Phytoecdysteroids: biological effects, application in agriculture and complementary medicine (as presented at the 14-th Ecdysone Workshop, July, 2000, Rapperswil, Switzerland). Ukr Biokhim Zh. 2001 May-Jun;73(3):21-9.

"The signaling pathway by which ecdysterone may coregulate the $O_2(-)$ and NO generation in heart mitochondria of aging rats may involve an outer mitochondrial membrane estrogen receptor coupled to mitochondrial PI3K/Akt/PKB activation results in superactivation and constitutive NO synthesis by mtcNOS."

Sahach VF, Korkach IuP, Kotsiuruba AV, Rudyk OV, Vavilova HL. Mitochondrial permeability transition pore opening inhibition by ecdysterone in heart mitochondria of aging rats. Fiziol Zh. 2008;54(4):3-10.

20-Ecd → ↑Ca^{2+} → PI3K → AKT → mTORC1 → RNA Translation → Muscle Growth

Athletes are always curious about testosterone. Young athletes ask me on a regular basis about anabolic steroids- if they're really as good as promoted, if they are harmful, and where can they get some! I remind these athletes that they make all the 'homegrown" testosterone they need when they train with intensity, and that other factors within the anabolic pathway (such as protein translation) can be enhanced naturally for superior results. A lot has been learned just recently about how testosterone works via signal transduction pathways. Testosterone is more than a "male sex hormone". It is an important contributor to the robust metabolic functioning of multiple bodily systems.

What testosterone turns on to build muscle has been answered. Below are some abstract summaries of some of this research. Notice that a main role of testosterone is to switch on the very same non-hormonal anabolic pathways that you've been reading about in regard to nutrient ergogenic anabolic activity. I'm confident that the synergy that can be created through the methodical use of nutrient ergogenics with non-hormonal anabolic action via mTORC1 will create all the growth in muscle mass, strength, and explosiveness you or your athlete will ever need.

"Low endogenous testosterone production, known as hypogonadism is commonly associated with conditions inducing muscle wasting. Akt signaling can control skeletal muscle mass through mTOR regulation of protein synthesis and FoxO regulation of protein degradation, and this pathway has been previously identified as a target of androgen signaling."

"Testosterone (T) sensitivity of Akt/mTORC1 signaling was examined in C(2)C(12) myotubes, and mTOR phosphorylation was induced independent of Akt activation at low T concentrations, while a higher T concentration was required to activate Akt signaling. Interestingly, low concentration T was sufficient to amplify myotube mTOR and Akt signaling after 24 h of T withdrawal, demonstrating the potential in cultured myotubes for a T initiated positive feedback mechanism to amplify Akt/mTOR signaling. In summary, androgen withdrawal decreases muscle myofibrillar protein synthesis through Akt/mTORC1 signaling, which is independent of AMPK activation, and readily reversible by anabolic steroid administration. Acute Akt activation in C(2)C(12) myotubes is sensitive to a high concentration of testosterone, and low concentrations of testosterone can activate mTOR signaling independent of Akt."

White JP, Gao S, Puppa MJ, Sato S, Welle SL, Carson JA. Testosterone regulation of Akt/mTORC1/FoxO3a signaling in skeletal muscle. Mol Cell Endocrinol. 2013 Jan 30;365(2):174-86. "The present study demonstrates testosterone administration improves hypertrophy in myoblasts that basally display impaired differentiation and hypertrophic capacity vs. their parental controls, the action of testosterone in this model was mediated by PI3K/Akt pathway."

Deane CS, Hughes DC, Sculthorpe N, Lewis MP, Stewart CE, Sharples AP. Impaired hypertrophy in myoblasts is improved with testosterone administration. J Steroid Biochem Mol Biol. 2013 May 25;138C:152-161.

"Testosterone increases the size and strength of skeletal muscle. This study further characterized the molecular mechanisms of the anabolic actions of testosterone on a rat myoblast cell line (L6 cells). Testosterone did not induce hypertrophy in L6 cells lacking the androgen receptor (AR). Hypertrophy was prevented by the AR antagonist bicalutamide and the mTOR inhibitor rapamycin. Testosterone induced Erk phosphorylation by 2h, and mTOR autophosphorylation was elevated within 20min; phosphorylation of p70S6 kinase was increased by 2h."

"These findings indicate that testosterone stimulates hypertrophy of L6 myoblasts through a mechanism that requires its binding to the AR and involves a signaling cascade dependent upon Erk and mTOR which is likely activated by substances released into the extracellular space which are not IGF-1 or other ligands for receptor tyrosine kinases."

Wu Y, Bauman WA, Blitzer RD, Cardozo C. Testosterone-induced hypertrophy of L6 myoblasts is dependent upon Erk and mTOR. Biochem Biophys Res Commun. 2010 Oct 1;400(4):679-83.

ADDITIONAL NUTRITIONAL ANABOLIC ERGOGENICS

The above listed ergogenic nutrients are among the most thoroughly researched nutrients that primarily influence the main anabolic pathway mTORC1 in a nutrigenomic way. There are other nutrients that are now being explored for potential anabolic mechanisms via mTORC1 and I have listed them. They may potentially be additional ingredients for use to repair, restore, and/or build skeletal muscle.

ARGININE

An amino acid shown to increase nitric oxide became a bodybuilding sensation when Medical Research Institute (MRI) first marketed this amino acid for what they termed "hemodiltion" and "the perpetual pump." Today there are dozens of supplements that tout the use of arginine in strength training to increase blood flow. While there is little if any research to support this claim, there is new published science to support the nutrigenomic action of arginine in the mTORC1 pathway. Arginine may work in synergy with leucine to stimulate the mTORC1 pathway.

Bauchart-Thevret C, Cui L, Wu G, Burrin DG. Arginine-induced stimulation of protein synthesis and survival in IPEC-J2 cells is mediated by mTOR but not nitric oxide. Am J Physiol Endocrinol Metab. 2010 Dec;299(6):E899-909.

Mejía-García TA, Portugal CC, Encarnação TG, Prado MA, Paes-de-Carvalho R. Nitric oxide regulates AKT phosphorylation and nuclear translocation in cultured retinal cells. Cell Signal. 2013 Aug 17;25(12):2424-2439.

Kim J, Song G, Wu G, Gao H, Johnson GA, Bazer FW. Arginine, leucine, and glutamine stimulate proliferation of porcine trophectoderm cells through the MTOR-RPS6K-RPS6-EIF4EBP1 signal transduction pathway. Biol Reprod. 2013 May 2;88(5):113.

Kong X, Tan B, Yin Y, Gao H, Li X, Jaeger LA, Bazer FW, Wu G. L-Arginine stimulates the mTOR signaling pathway and protein synthesis in porcine trophectoderm cells. J Nutr Biochem. 2012 Sep;23(9):1178-83.

González IM, Martin PM, Burdsal C, Sloan JL, Mager S, Harris T, Sutherland AE. Leucine and arginine regulate trophoblast motility through mTOR-dependent and independent pathways in the preimplantation mouse embryo. Dev Biol. 2012 Jan 15;361(2):286-300.

Tan B, Yin Y, Kong X, Li P, Li X, Gao H, Li X, Huang R, Wu G. L-Arginine stimulates proliferation and prevents endotoxin-induced death of intestinal cells. Amino Acids. 2010 Apr;38(4):1227-35.

URSOLIC ACID

Ursolic acid is a phytochemical found in plants. It is the major waxy component in apple skins. For commercial use it is often extracted from the herbs rosemary or thyme.

Steven Kunkel from the University of Iowa was investigating ursolic acids influence on muscle atrophy when he hypothesized that it might promote muscle growth in the absence of an atrophy-inducing stress. To test this, his team studied mice and discovered that compared to mice on the control diet, mice receiving ursolic acid possessed larger skeletal muscles, larger skeletal muscle fibers, and increased grip strength. Dietary ursolic acid was shown to increase the specific force generated by muscles.

Taken together, Kunkel's data suggest that ursolic acid first enhances the capacity of preexisting IGF-I and insulin to activate skeletal muscle IGF-I receptors and insulin receptors, respectively. Importantly, ursolic acid alone was not sufficient to increase activation of the IGF-I receptor or insulin receptor. Rather, its effects also required IGF-I and insulin, respectively. This suggests that ursolic acid inhibits receptor deactivation.

"A natural compound enriched in apples, ursolic acid reduced muscle atrophy and stimulated muscle hypertrophy in mice. It did so by enhancing skeletal muscle insulin/IGF-I signaling, and inhibiting atrophy-associated skeletal muscle mRNA expression. Importantly, ursolic acid's effects on muscle were accompanied by reductions in adiposity, fasting blood glucose and plasma cholesterol and triglycerides."

Kunkel SD, Suneja M, Ebert SM, Bongers KS, Fox DK, Malmberg SE, Alipour F, Shields RK, Adams CM. mRNA expression signatures of human skeletal muscle atrophy identify a natural compound that increases muscle mass. Cell Metab. 2011 Jun 8;13(6):627-38.

Kunkel SD, Elmore CJ, Bongers KS, Ebert SM, Fox DK, Dyle MC, Bullard SA, Adams CM. Ursolic acid increases skeletal muscle and brown fat and decreases diet-induced obesity, glucose intolerance and fatty liver disease. PLoS One. 2012;7(6):e39332.

"A recent study identified ursolic acid (UA) as a potent stimulator of muscle protein anabolism via PI3K/Akt signaling, thereby suggesting that UA can increase Akt-independent mTOR complex 1 (mTORC1) activation induced by resistance exercise via Akt signaling. The purpose of the present study was to investigate the effect of UA on resistance exercise-induced mTORC1 activation."

"These results indicate that UA is able to sustain resistance exercise-induced mTORC1 activity."

Ogasawara R, Sato K, Higashida K, Nakazato K, Fujita S. Ursolic acid stimulates mTORC1 signaling after resistance exercise in rat skeletal muscle. Am J Physiol Endocrinol Metab. 2013 Sep;305(6):E760-5.

Ursolic Acid → Insulin & IGF-1 Receptor Activation → IRS1 → PI3K → AKT → mTORC1

Ursolic acid has hormetic effects. I've worked with it for ten years to prevent sarcopenia (muscle loss in the elderly) in aging individuals. It's useful in small doses but toxic at larger doses. To increase insulin and IGF-1 receptor activity which then stimulates the mTORC1 pathway in athletes requires some research to see where an effective dose falls.

CITRULLINE

One final nutrient I've included in the anabolic ergogenic section is an amino acid called citrulline. It's a key intermediate in the bodies urea cycle which helps to excrete excess ammonia. Citrulline is made from ornithine and arginine. It is commonly sold as citrulline malate which is the amino acid bound to the fruit acid malic acid. I'm sure you will soon see citrulline bound to all kinds of substances as supplement companies make an all too common attempt to grab a marketing edge.

As you read below, citrulline can boost mTORC1 activity and thus skeletal muscle protein synthesis, but the question is, by how much and is this better than EAA's and leucine? I think the answer is no. As far as any synergy with leucine, this has not been studied yet.

Citrulline also converts to the amino acid arginine which has been promoted in the bodybuilding magazines for some time to increase nitric oxide and hypothetically (although unproven) muscle pump and delivery of nutrients.

"Both leucine and citrulline stimulate muscle protein synthesis, in part through a common mechanism of action mediated by the mTOR signaling pathway. Both leucine- and citrulline-enriched diets improve nutritional status in various experimental models of injury."

Cynober L, de Bandt JP, Moinard C. Leucine and citrulline: two major regulators of protein turnover. World Rev Nutr Diet. 2013;105:97-105.

"Citrulline possesses a highly specific metabolism that bypasses splanchnic extraction because it is not used by the intestine or taken up by the liver. The administration of citrulline may be used to deliver available nitrogen for protein homeostasis in peripheral tissues and as an arginine precursor synthesized de novo in the kidneys and endothelial and immune cells. Several pharmacokinetic studies have confirmed that citrulline is efficiently absorbed when administered orally. Oral citrulline could be used to deliver arginine to the systemic circulation or as a protein anabolic agent in specific clinical situations, because recent data have suggested that citrulline, although not a component of proteins, stimulates protein synthesis in skeletal muscle through the mammalian target of rapamycin signaling pathway. Hence, citrulline could play a pivotal role in maintaining protein homeostasis and is a promising pharmaconutrient in nutritional support strategies for malnourished patients, especially in aging and sarcopenia."

Bahri S, Zerrouk N, Aussel C, Moinard C, Crenn P, Curis E, Chaumeil JC, Cynober L, Sfar S. Citrulline: from metabolism to therapeutic use. Nutrition. 2013 Mar;29(3):479-84.

"Leucine (LEU) is recognized as a major regulator of muscle protein synthesis (MPS). Citrulline (CIT) is emerging as a potent new regulator. The aim of our study was to compare MPS modulation by CIT and LEU in food-deprived rats and to determine whether their action was driven by similar mechanisms."

"LEU and CIT administration differently stimulated the mTORC1 pathway (LEU > CIT). LEU but not CIT increased the phosphorylation of rpS6 at serine 235/236. Our findings clearly demonstrated that both CIT and LEU were able to stimulate MPS, but this effect was likely related to the nitrogen load. LEU, CIT and NEAA may have different actions on MPS in this model as they share different mTORC1 regulation capacities."

Le Plénier S, Walrand S, Noirt R, Cynober L, Moinard C. Effects of leucine and citrulline versus non-essential amino acids on muscle protein synthesis in fasted rat: a common activation pathway? Amino Acids. 2012 Sep;43(3):1171-8.

Citruline malate may be more effective at improving blood flow than the amino acid l-arginine or its derivatives, because l-arginine is easily degraded by normal metabolic processes and citrulline is not degraded, which means it has a better chance of increasing nitric oxide for improved blood flow. Citrulline turns into arginine after absorption.

In contrast to all the "perpetual pump" marketing efforts by sport supplement companies over the past several years, I'm not sure these compounds make much difference to athletes. Even though these supplements are promoted to boost nitric oxide (NO) there is extensive science to show they have little if any benefit on performance.

"To test the efficacy and safety of oral L-citrulline supplementation in improving erection hardness in patients with mild erectile dysfunction (ED). L-arginine supplementation improves nitric oxide-mediated vasodilation and endothelial function; however, oral administration has been hampered by extensive presystemic metabolism. In contrast, L-citrulline escapes presystemic metabolism and is converted to L-arginine, thus setting the rationale for oral L-citrulline supplementation as a donor for the L-arginine/nitric oxide pathway of penile erection."

"A total of 24 patients, mean age 56.5 ± 9.8 years, were entered and concluded the study without adverse events. The improvement in the erection hardness score from 3 (mild ED) to 4 (normal erectile function) occurred in 2 (8.3%) of the 24 men when taking placebo and 12 (50%) of the 24 men when taking L-citrulline (P < .01)."

"Although less effective than phosphodiesterase type-5 enzyme inhibitors, at least in the short term, L-citrulline supplementation has been proved to be safe and psychologically well accepted by patients. Its role as an alternative treatment for mild to moderate ED, particularly in patients with a psychologically fear of phosphodiesterase type-5 enzyme inhibitors, deserves further research."

Cormio L, De Siati M, Lorusso F, Selvaggio O, Mirabella L, Sanguedolce F, Carrieri G. Oral L-citrulline supplementation improves erection hardness in men with mild erectile dysfunction. Urology. 2011 Jan;77(1):119-22.

"CM supplementation did not affect PCr/ATP ratio, [PCr], [Pi], [ATP] and intracellular pH at rest. During the stimulation period, it lead to a 23% enhancement of specific force production that was associated to significant decrease in both PCr (28%) and oxidative (32%) costs of contraction, but had no effect on the time-courses of phosphorylated compounds and intracellular pH. Furthermore, both the rate of PCr resynthesis during the post-stimulation period (VPCr(rec)) and the oxidative ATP synthesis capacity (Q(max)) remained unaffected by CM treatment. These data demonstrate that CM supplementation under healthy condition has an ergogenic effect associated to an improvement of muscular contraction efficiency."

Giannesini B, Le Fur Y, Cozzone PJ, Verleye M, Le Guern ME, Bendahan D. Citrulline malate supplementation increases muscle efficiency in rat skeletal muscle. Eur J Pharmacol. 2011 Sep 30;667(1-3):100-4.

"The purpose of the present study was to determine the effects of a single dose of citrulline malate (CM) on the performance of flat barbell bench presses as an anaerobic exercise and in terms of decreasing muscle soreness after exercise. Forty-one men performed 2 consecutive pectoral training session protocols (16 sets). The study was performed as a randomized, double-blind, 2-period crossover design. Eight grams of CM was used in 1 of the 2 training sessions, and a placebo was used in the other. The subjects' resistance was tested using the repetitions to fatigue test, at 80% of their predetermined 1 repetition maximum (RM), in the 8 sets of flat barbell bench presses during the pectoral training session (S1-4 and S1'-4'). The p-value was 0.05. The number of repetitions showed a significant increase from placebo treatment to CM treatment from the third set evaluated (p <0.0001). This increase was positively correlated with the number of sets, achieving 52.92% more repetitions and the 100% of response in the last set (S4'). A significant decrease of 40% in muscle soreness at 24 hours and 48 hours after the pectoral training session and a higher percentage response than 90% was achieved with CM supplementation. The only side effect reported was a feeling of stomach discomfort in 14.63% of the subjects. We conclude that the use of CM might be useful to increase athletic performance in high-intensity anaerobic exercises with short rest times and to relieve post-exercise muscle soreness. Thus, athletes undergoing intensive preparation involving a high level of training or in competitive events might profit from CM."

Pérez-Guisado J, Jakeman PM. Citrulline malate enhances athletic anaerobic performance and relieves muscle soreness. J Strength Cond Res. 2010 May;24(5):1215-22.

"Protein energy malnutrition is common in the elderly, especially in hospitalized patients. The development of strategies designed to correct such malnutrition is essential. Our working hypothesis was that poor response to nutrition with advancing age might be related to splanchnic sequestration of amino acids, which implies that fewer amino acids reach the systemic circulation. Administration of citrulline, which is not taken up by the liver, can offer a means of increasing whole body nitrogen availability and, hence, improve nutritional status."

"The ASR were 0.30 +/- 0.04, 0.31 +/- 0.04, and 0.56 +/- 0.10 mg/h in the three groups, respectively (R and NEAA vs. Cit, $P < 0.05$). Insulinemia was significantly higher in the Cit group. For the first time, a realistic therapeutic approach is proposed to improve muscle protein content in muscle in frail state related to malnutrition in aging."

Osowska S, Duchemann T, Walrand S, Paillard A, Boirie Y, Cynober L, Moinard C. Citrulline modulates muscle protein metabolism in old malnourished rats. Am J Physiol Endocrinol Metab. 2006 Sep;291(3):E582-6.

"Previous studies have shown an antiasthenic effect of citrulline/malate (CM) but the mechanism of action at the muscular level remains unknown. Eighteen men complaining of fatigue but with no documented disease were included in the study. A rest-exercise (finger flexions)-recovery protocol was performed twice before (D-7 and D0), three times during (D3, D8, D15), and once after (D22) 15 days of oral supplementation with 6 g/day CM. Metabolism of the flexor digitorum superficialis was analysed by $(31)P$ magnetic resonance spectroscopy at 4.7 T. Metabolic variables measured twice before CM ingestion showed no differences, indicating good reproducibility of measurements and no learning effect from repeating the exercise protocol. CM ingestion resulted in a significant reduction in the sensation of fatigue, a 34% increase in the rate of oxidative ATP production during exercise, and a 20% increase in the rate of phosphocreatine recovery after exercise, indicating a larger contribution of oxidative ATP synthesis to energy production. Considering subjects individually and variables characterising aerobic function, extrema were measured after either eight or 15 days of treatment, indicating chronological heterogeneity of treatment induced changes. One way analysis of variance confirmed improved aerobic function, which may be the result of an enhanced malate supply activating ATP production from the tricarboxylic acid cycle through anaplerotic reactions. The changes in muscle metabolism produced by CM treatment indicate that CM may promote aerobic energy production."

Bendahan D, Mattei JP, Ghattas B, Confort-Gouny S, Le Guern ME, Cozzone PJ. Citrulline/malate promotes aerobic energy production in human exercising muscle. Br J Sports Med. 2002 Aug;36(4):282-9.

"Oral L-arginine supplementation has been shown to improve treadmill time to exhaustion and resting insulin sensitivity in individuals with peripheral vascular disease and type 2 diabetes, respectively. Furthermore, L-citrulline supplementation increases plasma L-arginine concentration to a level higher than that achieved by oral L-arginine supplementation. The purpose of this investigation was therefore to determine whether time to exhaustion during a graded treadmill test, as well as plasma insulin and glucose profiles, could be improved with oral L-citrulline supplementation in healthy individuals."

"It can be concluded that, contrary to the hypothesized improvement in treadmill time following L-citrulline ingestion, there is a reduction in treadmill time following L-citrulline ingestion over the 24 h prior to testing. The normal response of increased plasma insulin following high-intensity exercise is also not present in the L-citrulline condition, indicating that L-citrulline ingestion may reduce nitric oxide-mediated pancreatic insulin secretion or increased insulin clearance."

Hickner RC, Tanner CJ, Evans CA, Clark PD, Haddock A, Fortune C, Geddis H, Waugh W, McCammon M. L-citrulline reduces time to exhaustion and insulin response to a graded exercise test. Med Sci Sports Exerc. 2006 Apr;38(4):660-6.

"Dietary supplements containing L-arginine, a semi-essential amino acid, are one of the latest ergogenic aids intended to enhance strength, power and muscle recovery associated with both aerobic and resistance exercise. L-arginine is claimed to promote vasodilation by increasing nitric oxide (NO) production in the active muscle during exercise, improving strength, power and muscular recovery through increased substrate utilization and metabolite removal, such as lactate and ammonia. Research on L-arginine has recently tested this hypothesis, under the assumption that it may be the active compound associated with the vasodilator effects of NO. There were only five acute studies retrieved from the literature that evaluated exercise performance after L-arginine supplementation, three of which reported significant improvements. Regarding studies on chronic effects, eight studies were encountered: four reported enhancements in exercise performance, whilst four reports showed no changes. Whether these improvements in exercise performance - regardless of the aerobic or anaerobic nature of the exercise - can be associated with increases in NO production, has yet to be demonstrated in future studies. Low oral doses (≤20 g) are well tolerated and clinical side effects are rare in healthy subjects. In summary, it is still premature to recommend dietary supplements containing L-arginine as an ergogenic aid for healthy physically active subjects."

Álvares TS, Meirelles CM, Bhambhani YN, Paschoalin VM, Gomes PS. L-Arginine as a potential ergogenic aid in healthy subjects. Sports Med. 2011 Mar 1;41(3):233-48.

Olek RA, Ziemann E, Grzywacz T, Kujach S, Luszczyk M, Antosiewicz J, Laskowski R. A single oral intake of arginine does not affect performance during repeated Wingate anaerobic test. J

Sports Med Phys Fitness. 2010 Mar;50(1):52-6.

"I never learn anything talking. I only learn things when I ask questions."
~ Lou Holtz

"Don't force your kids into sports. I never was. To this day, my dad has never asked me to go play golf. I ask him. It's the child's desire to play that matters, not the parent's desire to have the child play. Fun. Keep it fun."
~ Tiger Woods

ENERGETIC ERGOGENICS

Athletes are often fixated on anabolic ergogenics, and rightfully so. But to build muscle and also make muscle perform in explosive sports the body requires specific sources of energy. There are many different forms of fuels to finally make ATP for the firing of the neuromuscular system. For explosive athletes, performance is predicated on how full the ATP stores are and how fast they are refilled to maintain explosive contractions.

Endurance trained athletes have adapted to using fats in skeletal muscle as major contributors to fueling performance. Endurance sports like long-distance running, cycling, and swimming can use muscle fatty acids, glycogen, amino acids and even lactic acid (lactate) to replenish ATP. Explosive athletes are different. Adapting to explosive training methods pretty much allows an explosive athlete to call on phosphocreatine and muscle glycogen reserves to quickly replenish ATP. Explosive athletes are not trained to use fatty acids as fuel which is why a weightlifter or a football player makes a lousy triathlete, and vice versa.

I love watching football and working with football players. I played on the offensive and defensive line in high school and while I focused on hammer throwing in college I've never stopped loving football. There's something special about being on the field during a Division I college or NFL game. What I especially like about football is the diversity in the athletes. Positions have different size, strength, speed, weight and height requirements. Yet all positions require similar traits like starting strength, maximal strength, power, reaction, fine motor skills, and striking force in various amounts at various times.

San Francisco 49er Joe Montana played in four Super Bowls and won them all. The only player in NFL history to be named Super Bowl MVP three times, Joe was inducted into the Pro Football Hall of Fame in 2000, his first year of eligibility. Brunner Photo.

Football play is performed with great speed and explosiveness. Example- the average NFL football game covers about 130 plays in less than eleven minutes of actual play. That's an average of 4.8 seconds for each play.

Football players are often timed in the 40 yard sprint. The NFL combine along with many college and high school teams use the forty as one test of talent. Running 40 yards during a play in football is rare. How many NFL offensive linemen run 40 yards on a play? The average NFL offensive linemen can run the forty in five seconds, some less and some more. The better linemen have superior starting power. It's tough to get a big (300+ pounds) engine moving from a stop. Success is often predicated on the first second of a play. That's where reaction time, starting strength, and explosiveness really shine- and that takes ATP along with a well-tuned nervous system. The only thing that is going to replenish this ATP right away is creatine phosphate (also called phosphocreatine or PCr), followed by muscle glycogen.

The Pre-Workout Supplement Boondoggle

So how can you increase your cellular PCr and muscle glycogen stores so that you have enough pre-fuel to boost ATP efficiently? The best way is to load the energy well ahead of needing it. Consuming a glucose polymer (maltodextrin) or sugar (glucose, fructose, sucrose, etc.) based beverage just prior to or during a training session when you are performing metabolically in an anaerobic way (not an aerobic way) will likely do nothing for your performance. You have to have the fuel in the tank well ahead of when you need it, not right before you need it, because it has to get absorbed, pass through the portal system (i.e. your bloodstream), get transported into the muscle cells, and then get stored or used right away. That's a tall order.

So sucking down a flavored pre-workout supplement or even one of the mass market flavored sugar/electrolyte drinks is really not going to do much if anything for you as far as performance, and may in fact reduce your performance and adaptive potentials depending on what is in the drink.

If after reading the above paragraph you've concluded that I'm not a big fan of pre-workout "performance" drinks, you are spot on. I've reviewed a whole bunch of them and I have some concerns with many formulas. First off, I'm not in favor of loading a whole bunch of ingredients into any supplement (my limit is usually six and they have to make sense- need, timing, synergy, useful dose, etc.) unless you really know how these ingredients perform together. Some ingredients cancel each other out, some are consumed at the wrong time, some are counterproductive, and some are just plain dumb. Many pre-workout supplements today contain over 20 ingredients. What could you possibly achieve from consuming that many ingredients? Many lead to a confused metabolism.

So why do sport supplement companies make pre-workout supplements? Because they simply want to fill a niche in the market- since many athletes have been mesmerized (I'd use the word manipulated but that may be too strong a word) that they need a pre-workout supplement to refuel, recharge, and pre-boost their metabolism prior to a workout. Nonsense. There is zero scientific validity to this assumption. Athletes have bought into the hype and sport supplement companies are only happy to oblige.

Many ingredients in these pre-workout supplements are questionable. Vitamins generally do not belong in supplements, especially the antioxidant vitamins C and E. If you see vitamin C in a sport nutrition supplement, question this products effectiveness right away. The manufacturer is not current with the science if they are adding C and E to a sport supplement. I'll detail why in a later chapter.

Ingredients like cinnamon extract and alpha-lipoic acid are added, I guess, under the pretense of improving blood sugar absorption into muscles. While these two ingredients may be appropriate for an overweight sedentary diabetic, it's doubtful they will have any positive influence on explosive performance in a well-trained athlete. They may in fact muddy the metabolic waters so to speak and dumb down mTORC1 and that would be a huge mistake.

Same goes for various forms of creatine prior to a workout. If we go by what almost twenty years of creatine science have taught us- that an athlete needs to either load it at 20 grams a day for a few days to boost creatine stores in muscle, or consume 5 grams daily for a couple weeks, then we know creatine needs some time to do its stuff. So how is downing a couple grams prior to a workout going to do anything? Crazy stuff!

Finally, I want to address the so called nitric oxide precursors like arginine HCL or AKG that are in many supplements. Where's the science with explosive athletes? For that matter, where's the science with bodybuilders? Dilating blood vessels to deliver more oxygen, energy, and nutrients to muscles is a noble quest, but you do this through muscle contractions already. It's usually not rate-limiting. Again, a well-trained athlete is not an out of shape old guy who needs a nitric oxide boost from a small blue pill. Just train with intensity and elicit strong muscle contractions and you will do very well.

Caffeine is also added to many pre-workout supplements. While caffeine has some good scientific support at increasing muscle power, throwing it in with a whole bunch of other ingredients is often done just so the athlete "feels" something during their workout. If you want to use caffeine I suggest you buy caffeine tabs and consume them prior to a competition. They are cheap and can be effective. I would not however consume caffeine on a habitual or regular basis as this seems to interfere with a natural adaptive long-term response to training.

I recommend you stick with water prior to, and during, your workouts. You aren't running a marathon. There is no reason to potentially disrupt your metabolism and burn through your cash by consuming a bunch of oftentimes useless ingredients as well as non-productive and questionable artificial sweeteners and flavors just so you can have your yummy pre-workout drink. Dream on!

If you or your team is under contract to consume a sponsor's flavored beverage, do so with hydration in mind but don't expect much more than this.

CAFFEINE

Caffeine used to be a banned substance but this ban was lifted in 2004. However, some have urged the re-banning of caffeine as an upper prior to competition. As of this writing caffeine is not banned, but as a competitive athlete you should always look at the banned substance list. The international banning and policing of banned substances is through the World Anti-Doping Agency or WADA. This agency works with national governing bodies to ensure legal and fair competitions. The ten page banned substance list as well as additional information can found at www.wada-ama.org.

Caffeine is a natural alkaloid present in the leaves, fruits, and seeds of various plants such as coffee, kola, tea, Guarana, Yerba Mate, and cacao (chocolate). In plants caffeine acts as a natural insecticide, preventing bugs from chewing on the plant. Caffeine can also be synthesized in the laboratory and is commonly known as anhydrous caffeine.

Generally, ingestion of between 1.4 and 4 milligrams for each pound of body weight has been repeatedly shown as ergogenic under several different types of exercise. A study by Del Coso and team looked at various ranges of caffeine use and their influence on half-squat and bench-press power production. They found that at least 3mg/kg (1.4mg/pound) of body weight were needed to influence maximal muscle power.

Del Coso J, Salinero JJ, González-Millán C, Abián-Vicén J, Pérez-González B. Dose response effects of a caffeine-containing energy drink on muscle performance: a repeated measures design. J Int Soc Sports Nutr. 2012 May 8;9(1):21.

Mark Tarnopolsky from McMaster University in Canada reviewed the research of caffeine on endurance activity. He writes that "there is no evidence that caffeine alters peripheral nerve conduction velocity of neuromuscular transmission" but adds that two studies "suggest that caffeine can enhance contractile force during sub-maximal contractions by potentiating calcium release from the ryanodine receptor (intracellular calcium channels), not by altering sarcoplasmic excitability" and "the ergogenic effects of caffeine during endurance activity are mediated partly by enhanced contractile force and partly by a reduction in perceived exertion, possibly though a blunting of effort and (or) pain."

Tarnopolsky MA. Effect of caffeine on the neuromuscular system--potential as an ergogenic aid. Appl Physiol Nutr Metab. 2008 Dec;33(6):1284-9.

In a study by the Italian sport researcher Dr. Illenia Bazzucchi and her team found that 6 milligrams of caffeine per kilogram (2.7mg/lb) of body weight improved performance during short-duration maximal dynamic contractions- with an improvement in muscle fiber conduction velocity and fiber recruitment.

Bazzucchi I, Felici F, Montini M, Figura F, Sacchetti M. Caffeine improves neuromuscular function during maximal dynamic exercise. Muscle Nerve. 2011 Jun;43(6):839-44.

In a study by Kathleen Woolf and colleagues from Arizona State University, eighteen male subjects (average age of 24 years) were given 5mg/kg of caffeine prior to an anaerobic strength/power test. Subjects lifted more total weight in the chest press and showed greater peak power during a Wingate test than those on a placebo.

Woolf K, Bidwell WK, Carlson AG. The effect of caffeine as an ergogenic aid in anaerobic exercise. Int J Sport Nutr Exerc Metab. 2008 Aug;18(4):412-29.

The same scientists followed up their earlier caffeine research with a study on the influence of caffeine on anaerobic performance of football players during an NFL Combine. They again administered a dose of 5mg/kg of caffeine. Compared with a placebo, there was no difference in performance in the 40-yard sprint, 20-yard shuttle, or bench press for reps.

Woolf K, Bidwell WK, Carlson AG. Effect of caffeine as an ergogenic aid during anaerobic exercise performance in caffeine naïve collegiate football players. J Strength Cond Res. 2009 Aug;23(5):1363-9.

This is an important study because it illustrates how top level athletes like these NFL Combine football players may not benefit anaerobically or neurologically from caffeine at the 5mg/kg dose as would a less experienced athlete.

I've seen such discrepancies before when comparing results between well-trained collegiate athletes (baseball, football, basketball and soccer) and professional athletes (MLB and NFL). Professional athletes are at the top echelon of explosive performance and their metabolism is fine-tuned. To elicit measurable improvements in the most elite athletes depends upon the context of training and competitive demands and may require a higher dose, a more complex synergistic formula, or may not be a rate-limiting factor at all.

Caffeine may also influence AMPK activity and PGC-1α by evoking calcium ion transients, triggering nitric oxide (NO) production. This is one way that caffeine may improve endurance by more efficiently burning fat as fuel via the AMPK and PGC-1α pathway.

Ding S, Riddoch-Contreras J, Abramov AY, Qi Z, Duchen MR. Mild stress of caffeine increased mtDNA content in skeletal muscle cells: the interplay between Ca2+ transients and nitric oxide. J Muscle Res Cell Motil. 2012 Oct;33(5):327-37.

In a study with team-sport athletes, researchers from Australia (Carr et. al.) tested the influence of caffeine on repeated (6 sets of 6 x 20 meters) sprint performance and reaction time. Their conclusion was that "caffeine ingestion 60 minutes prior to exercise can enhance repeated sprint running performance and is not detrimental to reaction time."

Carr A, Dawson B, Schneiker K, Goodman C, Lay B. Effect of caffeine supplementation on repeated sprint running performance. J Sports Med Phys Fitness. 2008 Dec;48(4):472-8.

In a follow-up study Carr and team tested the use of caffeine, sodium bicarbonate (baking soda, an alkalinizing compound to raise pH) or the combination of the two on power endurance. Eight well-trained rowers performed two baseline tests and four 2,000 meter rowing ergometer tests after ingesting 6mg/kg body mass of caffeine, 300mg/kg body mass of sodium bicarbonate, or both. While ingestion of sodium bicarbonate proved inconclusive, caffeine consumption alone increased rowing performance by about 2%.

Carr AJ, Gore CJ, Dawson B. Induced alkalosis and caffeine supplementation: effects on 2,000-m rowing performance. Int J Sport Nutr Exerc Metab. 2011 Oct;21(5):357-64.

In a study from Taiwan, researchers combined caffeine (6mg/kg BW) with creatine (300mg/kg BW) for five days and noticed a sizable increase in intermittent high-intensity exercise (10-second intermittent sprints on a cycling ergometer with

60-second rest intervals between sprints) over placebo or creatine alone. For an athlete weighing 200 pounds the dose for caffeine would be 550mg, and for creatine 27 grams.

Lee CL, Lin JC, Cheng CF. Effect of caffeine ingestion after creatine supplementation on intermittent high-intensity sprint performance. Eur J Appl Physiol. 2011 Aug;111(8):1669-77.

In summary: From the published science, a 5mg to 8mg per kilogram of body weight dose of caffeine seems functional for most athletes. Here's the breakdown:

Body Weight	Moderate Dose 5mg/kg	High Dose 8mg/kg
150 pounds (68kg)	340mg	544mg
170 pounds (77kg)	385mg	616mg
200 pounds (91kg)	454mg	728mg
220 pounds (100kg)	500mg	800mg

Takeaway: If you see a benefit in consuming caffeine for performance, try it out a few times prior to using before competition. Do not use habitually, meaning save its use for competitions only and not for training. Consume as a stand-alone and not in a mix with other ingredients to preserve purity and optimal dose management. Vivarin® caffeine tablets can be purchased through any pharmacy or online. A 40-count box of 200mg tablets costs about $9.

> *"Gold medals aren't really made of gold. They're made of sweat, determination, and a hard-to-find alloy called guts."*
> *~ Dan Gable*

MINERAL SUCCINATES

I mentioned mineral succinates toward the beginning of this book. Dr. Maria Kondrashova from Russia first began research on mineral succinates in collaboration with the famous Soviet anti-aging scientist Professor Vladimir Dilman. I met

Dr. Dilman during his visit to San Francisco in the mid 90's. He contributed toward a better understanding of oncology, endocrinology, and gerontology. Dr. Dilman was a pioneer in the neuroendocrine theory of aging and a co-author with Vladimir Anisimov who is the Head of the Department of Carcinogenesis and Oncogerontology at the N.N. Petrov Research Institute of Oncology, St.Petersburg, Russia. Dr. Anisimov has researched mTORC1 for some time.

I visited the institute in 1991 and spent some time with Dr. Anisimov to learn more about cellular energetics, restoration, growth, and aging. From my discussions with Dr's. Kondrashova, Dilman, and Anisimov I came to the conclusion that mineral succinates are useful for cellular energetics and of potential benefit to explosive athletes.

"An important role of anaerobic formation of succinate in anoxic and hypoxic states and the activation of succinate oxidation under hypoxia were shown. It was concluded that, for maintaining the energetics of animal cells under conditions of oxygen deficiency, it is advisable to use substrates capable of participating in the anaerobic formation of succinate, whereas under hypoxia it is reasonable to use succinate itself."

Maevskiĭ EI, Grishina EV, Rozenfel'd AS, Ziakun AM, Vereshchagina VM, Kondrashova MN. [Anaerobic formation of succinate and facilitation of its oxidation -- possible mechanisms of cell adaptation to oxygen deficiency]. Biofizika. 2000 May-Jun;45(3):509-13.

"It has been shown on Retzius neuron of the leech that after preintroduction of sodium succinate the reaction to synaptic stimulation expressed in increased frequency of the impulse activity proceeds more intensively than in the norm. In connection with the fact that against the background of succinate effect reaction to acetylcholine increases it is suggested that this very mediator is responsible for slower decrease of the impulse activity frequency at synaptic activation."

Sergeeva SS, Bazanova IS, Burgova MP, Kondrashova MN. [The role of succinic acid in neuron reaction to synaptic activation]. Biofizika. 1986 Jul-Aug;31(4):631-3.

"On the addition of succinate, the Ca^{2+} capacity of mitochondria is greater by 5–7 times and Ca^{2+} retention is more than 10 times longer as compared with different NAD-Dependent substrates."

Kondrashova MN, Gogvadze VG, Medvedev BI, Babsky AM. Succinic acid oxidation as the only energy support of intensive Ca2+ uptake by mitochondria. Biochem Biophys Res Commun. 1982 Nov 30;109(2):376-81.

Kondrashova MN, Chagovets NR. [Succinic acid in skeletal muscles during intensive activity and during rest]. Dokl Akad Nauk SSSR. 1971;198(1):243-6.

BETA-ALANINE (β-alanine)

Supplementation with β-alanine has been shown in some studies to improve athletic performance in some exercises such as cycling, running, rowing, martial arts, and football. It does this by reducing proton ions that often result in lactic acidosis. So β-alanine may function as an ergogenic nutrient when metabolic acidosis is the primary factor limiting exercise performance.

During high-intensity exercise, muscle glycogen is used to refuel ATP. This process, known as anaerobic glycolysis, results in the accumulation of lactate ions and hydrogen ions (H+) which increases the acid level in muscle. As this acid level rises (pH drops), intracellular buffering capacity can fail which has a negative influence on muscle function, ultimately impairing force production while speeding fatigue.

An increase in H+ disrupts the resynthesis of phosphorylcreatine (PCr) as well as inhibits glycolysis which disrupts muscle contraction in repetitive high intensity exercise.

Buffers in muscle, of which Carnosine (β-alanyl-L-histidine) is a major nutrient provides the first line of defense as muscle pH drops. Carnosine is a cytoplasmic dipeptide formed by bonding histidine and β-alanine in an enzyme reaction by carnosine synthase. The availability of β-alanine from synthesis of small amounts in the liver, or larger amounts from the diet (carnosine is in meat and is broken down into β-alanine during digestion), is the rate limiting factor in carnosine synthesis in muscle.

There are over one hundred scientific papers published on β-alanine use in exercise. The results of the studies are mixed, but it seems clear that some athletes training under certain methods will benefit from β-alanine to raise performance, especially power-endurance or the ability to elicit strong muscle contractions over repetitive efforts. As with other ergogenic nutrients, the use of β-alanine in sport must be put into context. So let's look at some the most current science on β-alanine and athletic performance.

A good deal of the science has been conducted by Roger Harris from England in the UK, so I will cite some of his research. Dr. Harris was also a pioneer in the research into the phosphagen system in exercise during the 1970's as a co-author with Eric Hultman and has conducted extensive study with creatine monohydrate in exercise. As for β-alanine use in exercise, Roger Harris along with his co-researcher Mark Dunnett have a financial interest in β-alanine as they co-hold a US patent #8067381, "Methods and compositions for increasing the anaerobic working capacity in tissues" which was assigned to the supplement contract manufacturer and raw material supplier Natural Alternatives International (NAI) of San Marcos, California. NAI sells β-alanine under the patent protected brand name CarnoSyn®, carnosine synthesizer to other companies for use in various brands of supplements. You can find Carnosyn® added to multi-ingredient powder drink mixes and capsule formulations, as well as a stand-alone ingredient.

In a study by Harris et.al, amateur soccer players were put through an intermittent exercise test known as Yo-Yo Intermittent Recovery Test Level 2 (YYIRTL2) where athletes cover a distance of 40 meters (2 x 20m runs between markers) at an increasing speed with 10 seconds of active recovery (2 x 5m walk) after each 40 meters.

According to Roger Harris, "YYIRTL2 is an exercise capacity test designed to last between 5 and 15 minutes and helps evaluate a player's ability to perform repeated bouts of high-intensity exercise with a large contribution from anaerobic energy sources." The test ends when the player fails to reach the finish line in a certain time, or if they stop due to voluntary exhaustion. YYIRTL2 is a good test for any sport where the athlete experiences brief bouts of intensity followed by short recovery periods. The decrease in muscle pH (making muscle more acidic) may be a key factor in fatigue during the Yo-Yo test.

Subjects consumed CarnoSyn® at 3.2 grams per day, provided in 800mg sustained release tablets (four times daily at 3-4 hour intervals), over a 12 week period.

The research team hypothesized that 12 weeks of consuming β-alanine significantly raised muscle carnosine levels as they found that athletes performing with a placebo showed about a 7% decline in performance while the CarnoSyn® group on average experienced about a 34% increase.

Saunders B, Sunderland C, Harris RC, Sale C. β-alanine supplementation improves YoYo intermittent recovery test performance. J Int Soc Sports Nutr. 2012 Aug 28;9(1):39.

Carnosine seems to contribute about 20% of the buffering in slow twitch muscle fibers and over 45% in fast twitch type IIb fibers. Carnosine is linked to the maintainance of ATP levels and also increases the calcium ion (Ca2+) sensitivity of the contractile components of muscle fibers and also helps to offset the decrease in Ca2+ as well as increase in H+ ions during high-intensity exercise.

Culbertson JY, Kreider RB, Greenwood M, Cooke M. Effects of beta-alanine on muscle carnosine and exercise performance: a review of the current literature. Nutrients. 2010 Jan;2(1):75-98.

β-alanine functions within the nervous system by functioning as a neurotransmitter or neuromodulator and has several binding sites to aid in learning of new information. With intense exercise to muscle failure, multiple taxed systems such as psychological, metabolic, and neurological may reduce performance. Ultra-intense exercise reduces intracellular ATP by up to 40% and also causes a near total reduction in phosphocreatine stores, plus a sizable rise in hydrogen ions (H+) which increases muscle acidity. Such changes compromise exercise and recovery rates and these multiply when successive bouts of super-intense exercise occur.

There are other intracellular buffers including bicarbonates, citrates, and proteins are under tight metabolic control. While in untrained sedentary persons, carnosine typically adds just 7%-10% to intracellular buffering capacity, during intense exercise in trained athletes it buffers acidity over a wide range and in both slow and fast twitch muscle fibers. This is because training increases intramuscular carnosine levels and buffering capacity in trained individuals as an adaptive process.

There are some studies where athletes consumed both β-alanine and sodium bicarbonate to buffer pH. These studies showed an additive effect on mean power tests such as a Wingate test. In a study by Gabriel Tobias and team, judo and jiu-jitsu athletes who performed best during an upper-body Wingate test ingested 6.4 grams of β-alanine and 500mg of sodium dicarbonate per kilo of body weight each day for four weeks. According to the authors, chronic BA (β-alanine) and SB (sodium bicarbonate) supplementation alone equally enhanced high-intensity intermittent upper-body performance in well-trained athletes (7%-8% boost). Combined BA and SB promoted a clear additive ergogenic effect resulting in a 14% boost.

Tobias G, Benatti FB, de Salles Painelli V, Roschel H, Gualano B, Sale C, Harris RC, Lancha AH Jr, Artioli GG. Additive effects of beta-alanine and sodium bicarbonate on upper-body intermittent performance. Amino Acids. 2013 Aug;45(2):309-17.

In another study by Kagan Ducker and team, total sprint times in athletes were achieved by sodium bicarbonate and lesser when combined with β-alanine. The use of β-alanine alone showed no improvement.

Ducker KJ, Dawson B, Wallman KE. Effect of beta-alanine and sodium bicarbonate supplementation on repeated-sprint performance. J Strength Cond Res. 2013 Mar 21. [Epub ahead of print]

There is a physical issue with β-alanine and also carnosine. At a dose of 10 milligrams of β-alanine for each kilogram (2.2 pounds) of body weight, individuals often experience symptoms of paraestheia which is a sensation of neuropathic pain that includes steady burning, flushing, itching and/or prickling of the skin (pins and needles) on the face, neck, hands, and buttocks. That's why a timed release tablet of just β-alanine may be the best way to go with this nutrient as it better mimics the spread-out absorption as found in the diet.

On the market you'll find many blended sport supplements which contain a diverse group of nutrients such as caffeine, β-alanine, carnitine, vitamins and minerals, and amino acids. In some of these the β-alanine level is 3 to 4 grams. Knowing that just a single gram of free β-alanine can cause neurological alarm, it doesn't make sense to consume such formulas. Throwing a whole variety of "goodies" into an artificially sweetened and flavored drink mix makes no sense to me scientifically or economically.

Looking at the totality of the published science on β-alanine, it's clear that there are many types of training that will not benefit from the nutrient, while other studies show a benefit to using β-alanine. Why are there such discrepancies? This is because tampering with the buffering system of metabolism is a tricky thing to manipulate. Ultra- intensity repetitious exercise produces a whole lot of H+ which greatly increases the acidity in muscle, ultimately causing failure. It would be easy to say that since β-alanine is designed to boost carnosine levels, which can then increase pH (more alkaline), that hypothetically this may improve performance sometimes. But maybe acidification during exercise is part of the adaptive response? Maybe if we interfere with this process by raising pH we actually interfere with the ability to get better. Maybe we should leave β-alanine to competition phases? I don't have the answers for you as there is more research to be done. I do know though that unless you want to jump out of your skin, you'd best consume β-alanine in 800mg to 1,000mg timed release tablets to prevent paraestheia.

D-RIBOSE

Bioenergetic pathways in muscle provide high-energy compounds that are required for cellular integrity and function. Increased cellular demand for adenosine triphosphate (ATP) or limitations in the rephosphorylation rate of adenosine diphosphate (ADP) can decrease the total adenine nucleotide pool which are constituents of the nucleic acids DNA and RNA. Total adenine nucleotide levels may be significantly decreased as a result of myocardial or skeletal muscle ischemia (restriction of blood supply to tissues), certain metabolic diseases, repeated intense skeletal muscle contractions, or repetitive high-intensity exercise.

D-Ribose is a naturally occurring pentose sugar. D-ribose must be phosphorylated to D-ribose 5-phosphate by the cell before it can be used. In athletics, consumption of D-ribose has the potential to improve ATP levels as well as DNA and RNA in protein synthesis. But this is like saying your 10 year old has the potential to play in the NFL. It's a long road between potential and productivity.

D-ribose has been on the market for over ten years. I think it has benefits to older persons with a weak heart muscle, but I'm not sure it has a functional use in athletics. It's good to think it does, but the science is just not there. Here's what some research studies have concluded about D-ribose in exercise:

"A healthy cellular system involves the maintenance of an intracellular metabolic balance. Reactive oxygen species (ROS) are constantly produced as a normal product of cellular metabolism; however, during situations of cellular stress, these levels can increase dramatically with the potential to cause deleterious cellular structural and/or functional consequences. There is a significant elevation in these ROS following stressful situations, such as ischemia, hypoxia, high-intensity exercise, and in many diseases. To combat these ROS, neutralizing endogenous enzymes, as well as exogenous antioxidants, can aid in minimizing their potential untoward cellular effects. Exogenous reducing antioxidant agents, such as vitamin C and/or E, play a role in addressing these formed species; however, recent research has suggested that fruit seed extracts may provide additional cellular benefits beyond their antioxidant features. Furthermore, supplemental D-ribose enhances the recovery of high-energy phosphates following stress and appears to potentially offer additional benefits by reducing radical formation. Specifically, during periods of hypoxia/ischemia, supplemental D-ribose may play an inhibitory role in the breakdown of adenine nucleotides, influencing the subsequent formation of xanthine and uric acid compounds; and thereby affecting the release of superoxide anion radicals. The combination of D-ribose with reducing antioxidants may provide a more optimal state of cellular protection during and following times of oxidative stress."

Addis P, Shecterle LM, St Cyr JA. Cellular protection during oxidative stress: a potential role for D-ribose and antioxidants. J Diet Suppl. 2012 Sep;9(3):178-82.

What this study infers is that because D-ribose has some "antioxidant" effects by reducing radical formation that it's good for exercise. However, it is now well recognized that radicals, reactive oxygen and nitrogen species (RONS), in small amounts function as signaling triggers for adaptation to training. Mess with RONS at your own risk of reducing adaptation.

"The amount of adenosine triphosphate (ATP) stored in the muscle available for immediate use is limited, and once used, must be resynthesized in the muscle. Ribose, a naturally occurring pentose sugar, helps resynthesize ATP for use in muscles. There have been claims that ribose supplements increase ATP levels and improve performance. Other studies have provided mixed results on the effectiveness of ribose as an ergogenic aid at high doses. None of these studies have compared the impact of the recommended dose of ribose on athletes and nonathletes under exercise conditions that are most conducive for effectiveness. The purpose of this study was to evaluate the effectiveness of ribose as an ergogenic aid at the dose recommended for supplements currently on the market during an exercise trial to maximize its efficacy. Male subjects (n = 11) performed 2 trials 1 week apart. Each trial consisted of three 30-second Wingate tests with a 2-minute recovery between each test. Trials were counterbalanced, with 1 trial being performed with 625 mg of ribose and the other with a placebo. Peak power, mean power, and percent decrease in power were recorded during each Wingate test. Repeated-measures analysis of variance ($p > 0.05$) found no significant differences between ribose and placebo. These results suggest that ribose had no effect on performance when taken orally, at the dose suggested by the distributor."

Peveler WW, Bishop PA, Whitehorn EJ. Effects of ribose as an ergogenic aid. J Strength Cond Res. 2006 Aug;20(3):519-22.

"This study examined whether ribose supplementation before and during intense anaerobic exercise impacts anaerobic capacity and metabolic markers. Twelve moderately trained male cyclists

(22.3 +/- 2.2 y; 181 +/- 6 cm, 74.8 +/- 9 kg) participated in the study. Subjects were familiarized and fasted for 8 h after standardizing nutritional intake. In a double blind and crossover manner subjects ingested either a 150 mL placebo or ribose (3 g ribose + 150 microg folate). Subjects rested for 25 min and completed 5 x 30 s anaerobic capacity tests with 3 min passive rest. Six capillary blood samples were taken prior to and after sprints for adenine nucleotide breakdown determination. The experiment was repeated 1 wk later with alternative drink. Data were analyzed by repeated measures ANOVA. No significant interactions were observed for any performance or blood variables. D-ribose supplementation has no impact on anaerobic exercise capacity and metabolic markers after high-intensity cycling exercise."

Kerksick C, Rasmussen C, Bowden R, Leutholtz B, Harvey T, Earnest C, Greenwood M, Almada A, Kreider R. Effects of ribose supplementation prior to and during intense exercise on anaerobic capacity and metabolic markers. Int J Sport Nutr Exerc Metab. 2005 Dec;15(6):653-64.

In a study by Richard Kreider and Anthony Almada, 10 grams of oral D-ribose for five days did not affect anaerobic exercise capacity or metabolic markers in trained subjects.

Kreider RB, Melton C, Greenwood M, Rasmussen C, Lundberg J, Earnest C, Almada A. Effects of oral D-ribose supplementation on anaerobic capacity and selected metabolic markers in healthy males. Int J Sport Nutr Exerc Metab. 2003 Mar;13(1):76-86.

"This study used a randomized, placebo-controlled, crossover design to evaluate the effects of oral ribose supplementation on short-term anaerobic performance. After familiarization, subjects performed 2 bouts of repeated cycle sprint exercise (six 10-second sprints with 60-second rest periods between sprints) in a single day. After the second exercise, bout subjects ingested 32 g of ribose or cellulose (4 x 8-g doses) during the next 36 hours. After supplementation, subjects returned to the laboratory to perform a single bout of cycle sprinting (as described above). After a 5-day washout period, subjects repeated the protocol, receiving the opposite supplement treatment. Ribose supplementation lead to statistically significant increases in mean power and peak power in sprint 2 (10.9 and 6.6%, respectively) and higher (although not significant) absolute values in sprints 1, 3, and 4. In conclusion, ribose supplementation did not show reproducible increases in performance across all 6 sprints. Therefore, within the framework of this investigation, it appears that ribose supplementation does not have a consistent or substantial effect on anaerobic cycle sprinting."

Berardi JM, Ziegenfuss TN. Effects of ribose supplementation on repeated sprint performance in men. J Strength Cond Res. 2003 Feb;17(1):47-52.

In 4 gram doses for four times a day (16 grams) D-Ribose did not have a positive impact on post-exercise muscle ATP recovery or maximal intermittent exercise performance.

Eijnde BO, Van Leemputte M, Brouns F, Van Der Vusse GJ, Labarque V, Ramaekers M, Van Schuylenberg R, Verbessem P, Wijnen H, Hespel P. No effects of oral ribose supplementation on repeated maximal exercise and de novo ATP resynthesis. J Appl Physiol (1985). 2001 Nov;91(5):2275-81.

Does D-ribose replenish low ATP levels after intense exercise? In a study by Hellsten, Skadhauge, and Bangsbo, eight individuals performed cycle training consisting of 15 x 10 seconds of all-out sprinting twice per day for 7 days. After training they received either ribose (200 mg/kg body weight) or placebo, three times per day for 3 days. The results support their hypothesis that the availability of ribose in the muscle is a limiting factor for the rate of resynthesis of ATP. However, the reduction in muscle ATP observed after intense training did not limit high-intensity exercise performance. This means that a lower ATP level was not a rate limiting factor.

Hellsten Y, Skadhauge L, Bangsbo J. Effect of ribose supplementation on resynthesis of adenine nucleotides after intense intermittent training in humans. Am J Physiol Regul Integr Comp Physiol. 2004 Jan;286(1):R182-8.

While D-ribose has been heavily promoted by some sport nutrition companies there doesn't seem to be value to it under most if not all training situations. Some of the best exercise scientists have not found D-ribose to be effective. While the above study did show it had a positive effect on replenishing ATP levels, it may prove to be more valuable at helping to increase overall RNA translation activity in muscle protein synthesis, perhaps in conjunction with pyrimidines (6-Methyluracil) or a pyrimidine precursor (mineral orotates), but this is yet untested.

ATP BOOSTERS

Some nutrient companies have been experimenting on either delivery of ATP itself or nutrients that may increase ATP production to improve explosive performance. At this time such research is inconclusive. One nutritional on the market for a few years now consists of an ATP disodium salt. It goes by the branded name of Peak ATP®. The other nutrient elevATP® is derived from a soluble cold-water extract of trace minerals derived from ancient peat and combined with a polyphenol rich apple extract. Both have shown some positive results on untrained individuals, but as we all know, there's quite a metabolic leap from untrained to well-trained athletes. Whether or not these ATP boosting compounds will have any benefit to explosive athletes is yet to be determined.

"Sixteen participants (8 male and 8 female; ages: 21-34 years) were enrolled in a double-blinded, placebo-controlled study using a crossover design. The participants received either supplemental ATP (400 mg/d divided into 2 daily doses) or placebo for 15 d. After an overnight fast, participants underwent strength and fatigue testing, consisting of 3 sets of 50 maximal knee extensions performed on a Biodex® leg dynamometer."

"No differences were detected in high peak torque, power, or total work with ATP supplementation; however, low peak torque in set 2 was significantly improved ($p < 0.01$). Additionally, in set 3, a trend was detected for less torque fatigue with ATP supplementation ($p < 0.10$)."

"Supplementation with 400 mg ATP/d for 15 days tended to reduce muscle fatigue and improved a participant's ability to maintain a higher force output at the end of an exhaustive exercise bout."

Rathmacher JA, Fuller JC Jr, Baier SM, Abumrad NN, Angus HF, Sharp RL. Adenosine-5'-triphosphate (ATP) supplementation improves low peak muscle torque and torque fatigue during repeated high intensity exercise sets. J Int Soc Sports Nutr. 2012 Oct 9;9(1):48.

In a previous study using the same ATP nutrient but at a lower dose of 225mg saw a small ergogenic influence on muscle strength.

Jordan AN, Jurca R, Abraham EH, Salikhova A, Mann JK, Morss GM, Church TS, Lucia A, Earnest CP. Effects of oral ATP supplementation on anaerobic power and muscular strength. Med Sci Sports Exerc. 2004 Jun;36(6):983-90.

In an e-published study using elevATP® at a dose of 150mg, subjects showed an acute increase in blood levels of ATP by 64% along with a reduction in ROS (free radicals) and a small decrease in mTOR. This is surprising as one would expect mTOR to rise with an increase in ATP.

Reyes-Izquierdo T, Nemzer B, Argumedo R, Shu C, Huynh L, Pietrzkowski Z. EFFECT OF THE DIETARY SUPPLEMENT ELEVATP ON BLOOD ATP LEVEL: AN ACUTE PILOT CLINICAL STUDY. Journal of Aging Research & Clinical Practice. 2013 April; 13(51):1-7 e-published.

"I've missed more than 9000 shots in my career. I've lost almost 300 games. 26 times, I've been trusted to take the game winning shot and missed. I've failed over and over and over again in my life. And that is why I succeed."
~ Michael Jordan

LIPOLYTIC - THE BURNING OF FATS

As an explosive athlete, or a coach who trains explosive athletes, you already know that the main fuel your muscles use to power performance is ATP followed by phosphocreatine, followed by muscle glycogen. Fat doesn't come into the picture much unless your workout or competition is ultra-long and of lower intensity, which it likely is not.

The body has three ways of producing ATP: from creatine phosphate, anaerobic cellular respiration from glucose and aerobic cellular respiration from fatty acids, and lactate (produced from the glycolytic pathway. When oxygen is available after about two minutes of exercise, the pyruvic acid molecules from glycolysis enter the mitochondria where aerobic cellular respiration completely oxidizes glucose. This process is called the aerobic cellular response. This process of aerobic cellular respiration provides enough ATP for prolonged activity as long as sufficient oxygen and nutrients are available. Therefore, for any activity longer than 10 minutes the aerobic cellular respiratory system provides most of the ATP for longer endurance activities such as a marathon race.

Fat needs oxygen to be used as fuel; yet explosive athletes perform in a world with little oxygen. If you want to burn off excess body fat you've got to train differently than you do for your sport- but you should not train as an endurance athlete would, with lots of volume- training aerobically. Training aerobically like an endurance athlete will take away valuable time from training for your specific sport, place extra pounding stress on joints, and pirate your muscle.

You've learned at length about mTORC1 and its pivotal role in muscle growth during resistance training. The nutrients outlined in the anabolic section all have a pro-mTORC1 effect. Recall that he balancing pathway to mTORC1 is the AMPK pathway. While mTORC1 is increased when calories are ample, AMPK is active when energy is low.

When the ATP/AMP ratio drops, AMPK goes to work to allow for more ATP. So mTORC1 and AMPK are a balancing act. You need both and if you want to reduce excess body fat you have to tip the scales a bit toward AMPK- and how you do this is critical if you want to spare muscle and improve sport specific explosiveness.

Endurance exercise, like running long-slow distances will definitely trigger the AMPK pathway. So will fasting and so will certain nutrients from your diet. But as an explosive athlete who also wants to burn off some extra blubber you have to go about turning on AMPK methodically. You don't want to de-train your explosiveness, overstress your joints (long-distance endurance athletes often have knee and low-back problems as they age), or waste a bunch of time and take away from explosiveness training.

AMPK is the master pathway that ramps up mitochondria biogenesis (quantity and quality of mitochondria). One downstream protein from AMPK is Peroxisome proliferator-activated receptor gamma coactivator 1-alpha (PGC-1α).

Two metabolic sensors, AMPK and SIRT1 have been described in the science to directly affect PGC-1α activity through phosphorylation and deacetylation, respectively. While the physiological relevance of these modifications and their molecular consequences are still largely unknown, recent insight from different in-vivo transgenic models clearly suggests that AMPK, SIRT1 and PGC-1α might act as an orchestrated network to improve metabolic fitness. Metabolic sensors such as AMPK and SIRT1, gatekeepers of the activity of the master regulator of mitochondria PGC1α, are vital links in a regulatory network for metabolic homeostasis.

Performing exercise in a glycogen depleted state increases skeletal muscle lipid utilization and the transcription of genes regulating mitochondrial β-oxidation. Potential candidates for glycogen-mediated metabolic adaptation are PGC-1α and the transcription factor/nuclear receptor PPAR-∂.

Recent research suggests that a factor associated with muscle contraction and/or glycogen depletion activates PPAR-∂ and initiates AMPK translocation in skeletal muscle in response to exercise.

Philp A, Mackenzie MG, Belew MY, Towler MC, Corstorphine A, Papalamprou A, Hardie DG, Baar K. Glycogen Content Regulates Peroxisome Proliferator Activated Receptor-∂ (PPAR-∂) Activity in Rat Skeletal Muscle. PLoS One. 2013 Oct 17;8(10):e77200. (electronic online publication)

Fighting Excess Body Fat With Power, Not Endurance

At the start of the book I mentioned that the majority of my research the past decade has been focused on ways to improve the health of aging individuals. As we age we become metabolically inflexible. We stagnate. This stagnation is driven by dysfunctional muscle and especially the mitochondria inside muscle which is tasked with burning body fat for energy. When mitochondria are reduced in number and those left are not well-tuned, it's tough to burn excess fat.

Mitochondria that don't work so good burns fat inefficiently, kind of like a car engine that won't pass a smog check- they spin off a lot of free radicals (RONS) and these in turn activate the inflammatory response which creates more mitochondrial dysfunction over and over- a closed loop. So my research has been on how to get mitochondria working efficiently in aging men and women so they can burn off excess body fat while building important skeletal muscle which improves their vitality and balance.

The days of running laps, jogging on a treadmill, or endlessly oscillating on an elliptical machine to burn fat are over- yet in every health club in America you can observe folks doing endless exercise. New research conclusively shows that high intensity interval training (HIIT) is the way to go to efficiently burn off excess blubber, while staying explosive.

Let's be honest; wouldn't you rather be talking explosiveness than discussing fat loss? Most explosive athletes are lean, yet there are still a certain percentage of chubby athletes who can stand to lose a few pounds of the yellow stuff. I'll be brief on how to efficiently do this.

Traditionally most fat loss was focused on, well, fat folks, oftentimes really fat folks. Chubby explosive athletes aren't in the same category. They generally have a good foundation of explosive muscle but still carry too much fat. How to lose this fat while sparing explosiveness is the key. There are three integrated components to burning off excess fat while sparing functional explosive muscle: (1) AMPK/PGC-1α Activators; (2) Intermittent Fasting; and (3) Performing HIIT.

To burn fat you need to increase the AMP/ATP ratio. In other words, you need to starve ATP, to pull phosphates off for use as energy and not replace them. When you increase the AMP/ATP ratio you switch on AMPK. And when you switch on AMPK you activate PGC-1α which then increases mitochondria quantity and activity- which burns more fat.

1. AMPK/PGC-1α Activators

A number of natural compounds can trigger the AMPK pathway. Another well-known example of a hormetic process is exposure to low concentrations of certain phytochemicals. Humans appear to have evolved the ability to detect stress markers produced by plants in their habitats. A kind of "early warning system." In this way, humans prepare themselves in anticipation of potential adverse environmental conditions. This inter-species hormesis is known as xenohormesis, the phenomenon in which an organism detects the chemical signals of another species regarding the state of the immediate environment or the availability of food.

Plant based compounds; polyphenols in particular, are stress response chemicals in plants. They are produced when the plant experiences a stressor such as a bacterial, viral, or fungal infection, insect damage, excessive solar radiation, low water levels, etc. The more stressed a plant is, the more they manufacture these polyphenol protective compounds. When humans ingest these stress response compounds, slightly in excess of normal rates, certain stress response genes in us are activated, and this can include the AMPK pathway leading to a rise in PGC-1α and mitochondrial biogenesis which leads to more efficient fat loss.

There are over 5,000 different polyphenols in plants and most have not been studied yet in regard to triggering AMPK. But there are several commercially available polyphenols available that can enhance AMPK activity. I've cited a few studies below and there are many more. Polyphenols are often compounds of color such as the red skin of an apple, the yellow of turmeric, the purple of grape skins, the blue of a blueberry, or the orange of a habanero chili pepper. Some common "weight loss" supplements including green coffee bean, banaba, cocoa, fucoxanthin, green tea, and resveratrol all contain polyphenols which stimulate AMPK. Athletes can use these nutrients to help activate mitochondria via PGC-1α and burn more fat.

Ong KW, Hsu A, Tan BK. Chlorogenic acid stimulates glucose transport in skeletal muscle via AMPK activation: a contributor to the beneficial effects of coffee on diabetes. PLoS One. 2012;7(3):e32718.

Huang HC, Lin JK. Pu-erh tea, green tea, and black tea suppresses hyperlipidemia, hyperleptinemia and fatty acid synthase through activating AMPK in rats fed a high-fructose diet. Food Funct. 2012 Feb;3(2):170-7.

Cui X, Liu X, Feng H, Zhao S, Gao H. Grape seed proanthocyanidin extracts enhance endothelial nitric oxide synthase expression through 5'-AMP activated protein kinase/Surtuin 1-Krüpple like factor 2 pathway and modulate blood pressure in ouabain induced hypertensive rats. Biol Pharm Bull. 2012;35(12):2192-7.

Kurimoto Y, Shibayama Y, Inoue S, Soga M, Takikawa M, Ito C, Nanba F, Yoshida T, Yamashita Y, Ashida H, Tsuda T. Black soybean seed coat extract ameliorates hyperglycemia and insulin sensitivity via the activation of AMP-activated protein kinase in diabetic mice. J Agric Food Chem. 2013 Jun 12;61(23):5558-64.

Ueda M, Hayashibara K, Ashida H. Propolis extract promotes translocation of glucose transporter 4 and glucose uptake through both PI3K- and AMPK-dependent pathways in skeletal muscle. Biofactors. 2013 Jul-Aug;39(4):457-66.

Mukai Y, Sun Y, Sato S. Azuki bean polyphenols intake during lactation upregulate AMPK in male rat offspring exposed to fetal malnutrition. Nutrition. 2013 Jan;29(1):291-7.

Zygmunt K, Faubert B, MacNeil J, Tsiani E. Naringenin, a citrus flavonoid, increases muscle cell glucose uptake via AMPK. Biochem Biophys Res Commun. 2010 Jul 23;398(2):178-83.

Timmers S, Konings E, Bilet L, Houtkooper RH, van de Weijer T, Goossens GH, Hoeks J, van der Krieken S, Ryu D, Kersten S, Moonen-Kornips E, Hesselink MK, Kunz I, Schrauwen-Hinderling VB, Blaak EE, Auwerx J, Schrauwen P. Calorie restriction-like effects of 30 days of resveratrol supplementation on energy metabolism and metabolic profile in obese humans. Cell Metab. 2011 Nov 2;14(5):612-22.

I'm a big fan of the stilbene resveratrol use in fat loss. Stilbenes are a class of polyphenols found in many plants. A few years back scientists were looking for substances that could prolong health and longevity. They came upon resveratrol which was shown to increase enzymes known as Sirtuins. Sirtuin 1 (SIRT1) is the most heavily studied but there are seven of them. Sirtuins have profound stimulating effects on the AMPK pathway, helping to make mitochondria work efficiently and cleanly burn fat. This becomes more important as we age.

A word of caution about resveratrol and all other polyphenols: They are hormetic, meaning they are toxic at high doses, yet beneficial at low doses. Many of the dietary supplements on the market have an insanely high dose of resveratrol in them, sometimes as high as 500 milligrams. The marketing arm of the nutrition industry is founded on a "if a little is good, more must be better" mentality. This does not hold for many compounds, including stilbene polyphenols like those in Resveratrol that raise SIRT1 and other Sirtuins.

"The SIRT1 enzyme is involved in adipose tissue (AT) lipolysis. FOXO1 is a protein that plays a significant role in regulating metabolism. Adiponectin is an adipokine, secreted by the AT, which has been considered to have an antiobesity function. PPARγ is one of the key actors in adipocytes differentiation. This study was undertaken to investigate whether resveratrol can regulate SIRT1, FOXO1, adiponectin, PPARγ1-3, and PPARβ/δ in human AT."

"Ours results show that resveratrol modulates the studied genes, increasing SIRT1 ($p=0.021$), FOXO1 ($p=0.001$), and adiponectin ($p=0.025$) mRNA expression and decreasing PPARγ1-3 ($p=0.003$) mRNA in human visceral adipocytes."

"Resveratrol, in vitro and at low concentration, modulates genes that are related to lipid metabolism, possibly preventing metabolic disease in human visceral adipose tissue (VAT)."

Costa Cdos S, Rohden F, Hammes TO, Margis R, Bortolotto JW, Padoin AV, Mottin CC, Guaragna RM. Resveratrol upregulated SIRT1, FOXO1, and adiponectin and downregulated PPARγ1-3 mRNA expression in human visceral adipocytes. Obes Surg. 2011 Mar;21(3):356-61.

2. Intermittent Fasting

One of the three means of increasing the AMPK/PGC-1α pathway is intermittent fasting. In contrast to constant fasting which tends to disrupt the metabolic milieu and actually prevents fat loss, intermittent fasting can be quite effective. Restricting calories (energy) prior to high intensity intervals further amplifies fat loss (lipolysis) in recovery. Not taking in any calories for an hour after a HIIT workout will further increase lipolysis without compromising muscle mass or performance. In addition, an occasional half day (2-3 times a week) or full day (once a week) of fasting can be effective at maximizing the AMPK/PGC-1α pathway, again without reducing explosive performance.

In contrast, traditional means of reducing excess body fat have been focused on running long distance (even a mile is way too long for a football player) along with fasting for days at a time. Both are less productive and also pirate valuable explosive muscle and have a negative influence on performance.

Kitada M, Kume S, Takeda-Watanabe A, Tsuda S, Kanasaki K, Koya D. Calorie restriction in overweight males ameliorates obesity-related metabolic alterations and cellular adaptations through anti-aging effects, possibly including AMPK and SIRT1 activation. Biochim Biophys Acta. 2013 Oct;1830(10):4820-7.

In the following scientific abstract, men in a fasted state (no carbohydrates) were given a casein hydrolysate protein source (20g) prior-to, 10g during, and another 20g after HIIT training. Protein consumed without any added carbohydrate or fat calories seems to not interfere with the AMPK/PGC-1α pathway. I'm not sure that it is necessary to consume such quantities of protein within a HIIT window, but as far at AMPK it did not seem to have a negative influence. In contrast, I suggest you never consume carbohydrates prior to, during, or right after a HIIT training routine if you want to burn body fat. Carbs will definitely blunt the AMPK/PGC-1α response and turn off both mitochondrial biogenesis (the goal of HIIT) and lipolysis in short-term recovery.

"The aim of the present study was to test the hypothesis that consuming protein does not attenuate AMPK signaling when exercise is commenced in a glycogen-depleted state. After performing a glycogen-depleting protocol the evening before, the subsequent morning ten active men performed 45 min steady-state cycling at 50 % of peak power output (PPO) followed by an exercise capacity test (1-min intervals at 80 % PPO interspersed with 1-min periods at 40 % PPO). In a repeated measures design, subjects consumed 20 g of a casein hydrolysate solution (PRO) 45 min before exercise, 10 g during and a further 20 g immediately post-exercise, or an equivalent volume of a non-calorie taste matched placebo (PLA). Resting (PRO = 134 ± 29; PLA = 136 ± 28 mmol kg(-1)) and post-exercise muscle glycogen (PRO = 43 ± 16; PLA = 47 ± 18 mmol kg(-1)) was not different (P > 0.05) between trials nor was exercise capacity (PRO = 26 ± 9; PLA = 25 ± 10 min, P > 0.05). Phosphorylation of AMPK(Thr172) increased threefold immediately post-exercise (P < 0.05) and PGC1-mRNA increased sixfold at 3 h post-exercise (P < 0.05), though there were no differences between conditions (P > 0.05). In contrast, there was a trend (P = 0.08) for a divergent response in eEF2(Thr56) phosphorylation such that 1.5 fold increases post- and 3 h post-exercise in PLA were blunted with PRO, thus indicative of greater eEF2 activation. We conclude that athletes who deliberately incorporate training phases with reduced muscle glycogen into their training programs may consume protein before, during and after exercise without negating signaling through the AMPK cascade."

Taylor C, Bartlett JD, van de Graaf CS, Louhelainen J, Coyne V, Iqbal Z, Maclaren DP, Gregson W, Close GL, Morton JP. Protein ingestion does not impair exercise-induced AMPK signaling when in a glycogen-depleted state: implications for train-low compete-high. Eur J Appl Physiol. 2013 Jun; 113(6):1457-68.

Another paper by some of the researchers cited above shows the benefit to reducing carbohydrates before HIIT when they write "We conclude that the exercise-induced increase in p53 phosphorylation is enhanced in conditions of reduced CHO availability, which may be related to upstream signaling through AMPK. Given the emergence of p53 as a molecular regulator of mitochondrial biogenesis, such nutritional modulation of contraction-induced p53 activation has implications for both athletic and clinical populations."

Bartlett JD, Louhelainen J, Iqbal Z, Cochran AJ, Gibala MJ, Gregson W, Close GL, Drust B, Morton JP. Reduced carbohydrate availability enhances exercise-induced p53 signaling in human skeletal muscle: implications for mitochondrial biogenesis. Am J Physiol Regul Integr Comp Physiol. 2013 Mar 15;304(6):R450-8.

Aquilano K, Baldelli S, Pagliei B, Cannata SM, Rotilio G, Ciriolo MR. p53 orchestrates the PGC-1α-mediated antioxidant response upon mild redox and metabolic imbalance. Antioxid Redox Signal. 2013 Feb 1;18(4):386-99.

Saleem A, Carter HN, Iqbal S, Hood DA. Role of p53 within the regulatory network controlling muscle mitochondrial biogenesis. Exerc Sport Sci Rev. 2011 Oct;39(4):199-205.

3. High Intensity Interval Training (HIIT)

HIIT is an efficient and effective way for an explosive athlete to burn body fat. It activates the AMPK/PGC-1α pathway just like lengthy long-slow aerobic exercise does yet in much less time and friendlier to an explosive athlete's metabolism and neuromuscular requirements. A recent study compared HIIT with endurance running and concluded "We provide novel data by demonstrating that acute HIT and CONT running (when matched for average intensity, duration, and work done) induces similar activation of molecular signaling pathways associated with regulation of mitochondrial biogenesis. Furthermore, this is the first report of contraction-induced p53 phosphorylation in human skeletal muscle, thus highlighting an additional pathway by which exercise may initiate mitochondrial biogenesis."

Bartlett JD, Hwa Joo C, Jeong TS, Louhelainen J, Cochran AJ, Gibala MJ, Gregson W, Close GL, Drust B, Morton JP. Matched work high-intensity interval and continuous running induce similar increases in PGC-1α mRNA, AMPK, p38, and p53 phosphorylation in human skeletal muscle. J Appl Physiol (1985). 2012 Apr;112(7):1135-43.

Research by Martin Gibala and his team in Canada have shown the benefits of high-intensity low-volume HIIT in mitochondrial biogenesis. I've listed a full abstract from a paper they published in 2009. The key message they impart is that low-volume intense interval exercise takes little time yet is effective at ramping up mitochondria to burn fat.

"From a cell signaling perspective, short-duration intense muscular work is typically associated with resistance training and linked to pathways that stimulate growth. However, brief repeated sessions of sprint or high-intensity interval exercise induce rapid phenotypic changes that resemble traditional endurance training. We tested the hypothesis that an acute session of intense intermittent cycle exercise would activate signaling cascades linked to mitochondrial biogenesis in human skeletal muscle. Biopsies (vastus lateralis) were obtained from six young men who performed four 30-s "all out" exercise bouts interspersed with 4 min of rest (<80 kJ total work). Phosphorylation of AMP-activated protein kinase (AMPK; subunits alpha1 and alpha2) and the p38 mitogen-activated protein kinase (MAPK) was higher (P $\leq$ 0.05) immediately after bout 4 vs. preexercise. Peroxisome proliferator-activated receptor-gamma coactivator-1alpha (PGC-1alpha) mRNA was increased approximately twofold above rest after 3 h of recovery (P <or= 0.05); however, PGC-1alpha protein content was unchanged. In contrast, phosphorylation of protein kinase B/Akt (Thr(308) and Ser(473)) tended to decrease, and downstream targets linked to hypertrophy (p70 ribosomal S6 kinase and 4E binding protein 1) were unchanged after exercise and recovery. We conclude that signaling through AMPK and p38 MAPK to PGC-1alpha may explain in part the metabolic remodeling induced by low-volume intense interval exercise, including mitochondrial biogenesis and an increased capacity for glucose and fatty acid oxidation."

Gibala MJ, McGee SL, Garnham AP, Howlett KF, Snow RJ, Hargreaves M. Brief intense interval exercise activates AMPK and p38 MAPK signaling and increases the expression of PGC-1alpha in human skeletal muscle. J Appl Physiol (1985). 2009 Mar;106(3):929-34.

In a follow-up paper, Gibala added "A growing body of evidence suggests that high-intensity interval training (HIT) induces numerous physiological adaptations that are similar to traditional endurance training despite a lower total exercise volume and training time commitment. Low-volume HIT is characterized by brief repeated 'bursts' of vigorous exercise interspersed with periods of rest or low-intensity exercise for recovery. A common model employed in many HIT studies is the Wingate test, which consists of a 30 second 'all-out' cycling effort against a standardized resistance. In a typical training session, subjects complete four to six Wingate tests interspersed with 4 min of rest, for a total of only 2 to 3 min of maximal exercise spread over a ~15–30 min period."

Gibala MJ, Little JP. Just HIT it! A time-efficient exercise strategy to improve muscle insulin sensitivity. J Physiol. 2010 Sep 15;588(Pt 18):3341-2.

Action Plan

Have you ever seen a world class sprinter that was a little chubby around the middle? Of course not. They're muscular and ripped. This is what all explosive athletes should strive for. These sprinters do not spend time running laps to stay lean. They simply sprint at high intensity, with great muscle contractions, over-and-over. Just like HIIT.

High intensity intervals can be added to your explosive training program to burn more body fat while at the same time not interfering with your explosiveness. Basically HIIT is explosive efforts with good muscle contractions for short bursts and small rest periods, for a workout lasting between 15 and 30 minutes. You can also follow up HIIT with a weight training workout as HIIT does not take away from the anabolism of weight training.

There are many ways to program a HIIT routine. I personally prefer to do HIIT on a recumbent bike so I'll show you a routine for this. The bike I use has a monitor which shows all kinds of measurements. I set my body weight and time I want to bike for. If I'm doing a short workout I'll set the time for 15-20 minutes. I warm up at a lesser resistance for about five minutes and then increase the resistance a little so when I go into a sprint I can contract more muscle fibers. Now I go all out for a short sprint. I used to look at the time and sprint in a range of 10 seconds up to about 30 seconds, upon which I reduce the resistance a bit and pedal in a relaxed way for between 20 and 40 seconds. Then up the tension and repeat the sprint. There is no set magic time for the sprint or the relaxed pedaling. It's just what you enjoy and can handle intensity wise. I could also raise the resistance more but pedaling would be slower. Sometimes I change the resistance up or down and sometimes I keep it constant. Now instead of timing a sprint I often simply use my RPM's as a guide. When I first start a sprint my RPM's are somewhere around 120, and as I progress with the intense cycling the RPM's begin to drop. In a short while, say 30 seconds, plus or minus, the RPM's fall below 80 and this is when I reduce tension and cruise for a bit to get my breathing back. Then I go again.

You can also simply do intermittent short sprints and jogs around a track, or use a weighted sled (at a weight you can still drive with good speed and form) for short intermittent pushes, interspersed with a relaxed pushes or rest. The key is simply to perform short all-out efforts followed by a relaxed effort for a total time of between 10 and 30 minutes. For simplicity let's say you are going to do a 15 second high-intensity sprint followed by a 15 second relaxed effort and you are going to do this over and over for 20 minutes. This gives you two 15 second sprints each minute for a total of 40 high-intensity sprints in the workout (2/min x 20 minutes). Your total sprint time is just 10 minutes. If you do this right you will be gassed at completion but you will recover quickly so you can do some resistance training if you like.

The above scheme is just one example and is up to your creativity. You can do sprints lasting slightly longer; rest more between sprints, etc. You can do them on a bike, a treadmill, an elliptical trainer, on a field, around a track, or pushing a sled. Just think "high intensity intervals" where you give your all over short efforts. This will activate the AMPK/PGC-1α pathway and help you burn lots of fat but not take away from your explosive training.

To maximize the training effects do not consume calories prior to the workout. Never consume carbs for a couple hours before, during, or for at least one hour after a HIIT workout as this will bring AMPK/PGC-1α pathway activation and fat burning to a screeching halt. The workouts generally last no more than half an hour, and after HIIT you may be doing other training that lasts perhaps another 30 minutes to one hour. So chances are you can consume some protein a half hour after your total workout and then more protein with some carbs 3-4 hours later. The secret is to simply ride the AMPK/PGC-1α pathway after a HIIT workout and you can only do this if you go into the workout in a carb fasted state and you remain in a fast for a while after the workout.

You can also introduce some nutrients that further activate the AMPK/PGC-1α pathway. I prefer a polyphenol "cocktail" consisting of green coffee bean extract, green tea, and some resveratrol about a half hour prior to HIIT. This primes the AMPK pump.

Here's my final thoughts about HIIT, AMPK, and fat loss in overfat football lineman (or any athlete in any sport that's overfat). In many positions in football the athletes are generally muscular and lean. Yet on practically every high school football team you'll find an overfat athlete or two- usually a lineman. On many teams you'll find lineman lighter that they should for their position. The coach will tell them "you got to put on some weight" and so the young athlete because they are unsupervised, ends up eating all kinds of junk food to pack on the pounds. But now he's overfat and imbalanced. He has no sense of his body any more. Obese and overfat lineman in high school and college would be more explosive if they dropped the fat pounds and put on more muscle. Excess muscle fat actually blunts the anabolic response and makes gaining quality explosive muscle tougher. An athlete can lean out and build muscle during the same cycle- if they do HIIT.

The NFL is a different story. Every team has several huge linemen weighing in at 300 pounds plus. They struggle with their weight constantly. In order to keep up with their competition the thinking is that more mass, no matter whether it is muscle or blubber will win out. This is a fallacy.

Excess body fat is dysfunctional weight. NFL linemen generally carry between 20% and 30% body fat and at the upper end that's pretty high. It has no benefit to explosiveness and performance except for perhaps to cushion blows. Leverage, position, reaction, explosiveness and striking force will whip the fat guy every time. This is not to take away from the strength and power of an NFL lineman. They do pack a bunch of very powerful muscle. Powerful legs, hips and butt. But they're like a train engine trying, from a dead stop, to quickly pull a loaded coal car. It's slow to get started. That's what I see when I watch a game. Overfat lineman slow to get started and then slow to react.

But the reality is that coaches believe that this extra fat mass in the hips and butt are necessary to compete with the tubby lineman on the other side of the ball. I foresee a time in the near future when the new linemen are not only lean and muscular but also super-fast and reactive, at a body weight of 300 pounds and 12% to 15% body fat. And this will make a huge difference in their explosiveness. They will get there faster by following the ergogenic nutritional and HIIT recommendations in this book.

Sanford VS USC. Line play is always better from the field because you can feel the power. Brunner Photo.

ADAPTOGENIC

I first learned about adaptogens on my earliest trips to Russia between 1989 and 1992. Many of my Russian science colleagues during that time were aggressively studying adaptogens in the laboratory, searching for new compounds with adaptogenic activity, and conducting research on athletes. I can remember coming back to the states with a travel bag full of adaptogens in bulk, pill, and tincture form. Popular adaptogens at that time were Eleutherococcus, Aralia, Leuzea, Rantarin, Schisandra, Pantocrin, and moomyo. These were all used to increase endurance, physical working capacity, mental performance, fine motor skills, and modulate cortisol. Today many other adaptogens have been catalogued in pharmacopeia and they can be sourced from around the world.

Back in the 1940's, Russian scientist Nikolai Lazarev first defined an adaptogen as a substance that allows the body to counter adverse physical, chemical, or biological stressors by raising nonspecific resistance toward such stress. This allows the body to "adapt" to the stressful circumstances. The word adaptogen comes from the Latin word adaptare, meaning to fit or adjust.

Many adaptogens have been used throughout history as folklore medicines to help persons handle excessive stress. Much of the research on adaptogens has been conducted by Russian scientists and their findings lead to the practical use of plant and animal based adaptogenic substances in athletics, military operations, and also space travel.

When I think of adaptogens I think of an elixir or tonic- Substances that act as a tonic to the body which helps it remain in a healthy and productive zone during periods of stress. Adaptogens in sport can help an athlete train at greater volumes of high intensity overreaching exercise, recover quicker, and prevent overtraining.

Younger athletes generally are not pushing themselves to the limits of a major college, Olympian, or professional athlete, so I don't usually recommend most adaptogens for lower level athletes, although they likely may be of some benefit if the athletes intensity and volume is high. For elite athletes pushing the limits, especially during the competitive phase which can be long and hard to recover from, both physically and mentally, adaptogens can be of benefit to restore and re-balance.

I've worked with many different adaptogens over the years. What very few folks know until reading this book is that adaptogens are often toxic at high doses. They are stress response compounds which, at a low dose trigger your general stress response proteins to become stronger, kind of like exercise in a bottle.

Most athletes have no idea how to use adaptogens. They don't know which adaptogens to use, when to use them, at what dose, and for how long. There is no definitive answer to this as every athlete is unique and their training is special to them as well. One trick with adaptogens is to recognize that more is not always better. In fact, I generally recommend that athletes use adaptogens at a lower dose and then gradually increase the dose to find their hormetic limit. I covered the term hormesis earlier but to refresh, it's a process by which some stress (it can be chemical, physical, or emotional/ psychological) in a small amount is beneficial to the body, while that same stress in a large amount is toxic, harmful, or possibly deadly. You may have heard the expression "that which does not kill you makes you stronger" and in an adaptive way that's a hormetin, something in a dose one can handle without harm that nudges the body to become stronger and fight against stressors.

There is lots of adaptogen science and a whole bunch of adaptogens to choose from. It can be pretty confusing trying to select and use adaptogens in the right dose at the right times and definitely not as simple as many nutrition companies would lead you to believe. Adaptogens can have many compounds that influence the body in various ways, including having an inhibitory action against free radicals (i.e. RONS), anti-cancer, hypoinsulinemic, hypocholesterolemic, immunomodulatory effect, anabolic, antilipolytic, antihypoxic, etc. Some scientists have urged that the term "adaptogen" be dropped from the scientific literature because it is not descriptive enough as to the mechanisms of action. I agree with this. As I explained earlier, my research is focused on specific metabolic pathways which contain signaling proteins and enzymes that turn on various actions and turn off others. Thanks to the mapping of all the genes in the human body, scientists are now able to dig down into the workings of cells to the gene (DNA) level.

Among many discoveries within just the past ten years we now have a much greater understanding for example of how muscle protein synthesis is turned on and off, how oversized fat cells become stressed and cause inflammation, how free radicals spin out of control and age tissues, and how mitochondria become dysfunctional within a sedentary western lifestyle. This is why the new science is so important. If you're basing your training plan on sport or nutrition science that is even just five years old, you're missing out on great opportunities to become a better athlete thanks to new discoveries in the last few years- with even more soon to come. The science of nutrigenomics in human performance is exploding and yet still in its infancy.

Simply knowing that a nutritional, be it a plant extract like Rhodiola rosea, one from an animal like Rantarin (antler serum), or the ocean like fucoxanthin, is adaptogenic is not enough in today's more refined scientific arena. We must know how various extracts and their bioactive compounds influence our genes. Today we can do this but it takes more effort.

Adaptogens often have anabolic effects. They aid in rebuilding damaged muscle tissue following strenuous activity by facilitating the synthesis of protein via RNA translation within the body. Through the use of good adaptogens, the time needed for the body to recover from high-intensity training or extended periods of stress can be sizably reduced. I stress they must be good adaptogens.

My undergraduate degree is in agriculture and I've always had a love for plant chemistry. Some plants produce bioactives for health and physical performance, and organic growing methods which produce the best materials is an interest of mine. I've been able to associate with many scientists over the years and one adaptogen researcher and good friend of mine stands high above the rest. His name is Dr. Wudeneh Letchamo. Wudeneh grew up in the highlands of Ethiopia and received his masters degree in pharmacognosy (the study of medicines in plants) from Moscow Timiriazev Agricultural Academy in Russia, and his Ph.D. from Justus Liebig University of Giessen in Germany.

Dr. Letchamo is an interntional expert on plant based nutriceuticals and ethanobotanicals. He has worked extensively on the selection and growing of adaptogens in the USA, Canada, and Africa. His research has discovered that the quality of the adaptogenic materials from Russia and many other countries is of poor quality today. Plants have been over-harvested and quality materials today are in short supply. Because of this, many of the extracts on the market are of inferior quality. Some are even adulterated with inactive cheap materials that have zero adaptogenic activity. This is a big problem for athletes because if you want to take adaptogens to help you recover and adapt to heavy training loads you have to verify the quality. This is almost impossible without third party testing.

The fact is that much of the more common adaptogens like Rhodiola, Eleuthero, Holy Basil (Tulsi), and Ashwagandha have some serious quality problems. Manufacturers need to utilize third party testing to verify bioactivity so that athletes get a quality product.

Brekhman II, Dardymov IV. New substances of plant origin which increase nonspecific resistance. Annu Rev Pharmacol. 1969;9:419-30.

Panossian A, Wikman G. Evidence-based efficacy of adaptogens in fatigue, and molecular mechanisms related to their stress-protective activity. Curr Clin Pharmacol. 2009 Sep;4(3):198-219.

Panossian A, Wikman G, Kaur P, Asea A. Adaptogens exert a stress-protective effect by modulation of expression of molecular chaperones. Phytomedicine. 2009 Jun;16(6-7):617-22.

Holy Basil (Tulsi, Ocimum sanctum)

Holy Basil is a popular adaptogenic herb in Ayurvedic medicine. Research suggests that the anti-stress activity of Holy Basil is partly due to its antioxidant properties against oxidative stress. Compounds analyzed were shown to normalize a number of stress parameters including hyperglycemia, high cortisol, high blood fats, reduced cognition, adrenal stress, and reduced cell energetics. Holy Basil also has anti-inflammatory, analgesic and antibacterial activity. It has been shown to promote wound healing, promote cellular DNA stability during stress, and is a liver protector that works in synergy with silymarin (a standardized active) in milk thistle.

Holy Basil is one of my favorite adaptogens because it is mild and can be used just about any time, especially during long duration competitive periods such as a professional football, baseball, or basketball season. College age and high school age athletes can use it as well as it is a generalized stress modulator.

One of the main bioactive substances in Holy Basil is eugenol (also found in cloves) and some extracts are standardized for this compound, although there are many more beneficial compounds in Holy Basil. High quality Holy Basil is grown in India on small organic grown family farms. The best quality is achieved when the small plants are stressed by the monsoon (heavy rain) season from June to September, followed by high heat which stresses the plants further. This stress allows the plant to adapt by producing large amounts of actives, many in the oil, that are adaptogenic.

Holy Basil plants grown in a greenhouse, while they grow big, tall, and beautiful, are not stressed like those growing in the wild or under certified organic conditions. Holy Basil grown in a greenhouse is void of much adaptogenic activity. Remember, the actives in all adaptogens are generally stress response compounds, meaning when the plant is stressed it makes more to protect itself. When we ingest these stress response compounds, our cells go into alarm mode which ramps up our own cellular stress response genes.

If you decide to use Holy Basil, only use certified organic grown material because much of the material coming out of India today is grown using lots of fertilizers and pesticides to get the yield up. Just because the plant is big (high yield) is actually indicative of poor adaptogenic potency. The plants need to be stressed to yield the best material.

Jyoti S, Satendra S, Sushma S, Anjana T, Shashi S. Antistressor activity of Ocimum sanctum (Tulsi) against experimentally induced oxidative stress in rabbits. Methods Find Exp Clin Pharmacol. 2007 Jul-Aug; 29(6):411-6.

Gupta P, Yadav DK, Siripurapu KB, Palit G, Maurya R. Constituents of Ocimum sanctum with antistress activity. J Nat Prod. 2007 Sep; 70(9):1410-6.

Ahmad A, Rasheed N, Gupta P, Singh S, Siripurapu KB, Ashraf GM, Kumar R, Chand K, Maurya R, Banu N, Al-Sheeha M, Palit G. Novel Ocimumoside A and B as anti-stress agents: modulation of brain monoamines and antioxidant systems in chronic unpredictable stress model in rats. Phytomedicine. 2012 May 15; 19(7):639-47.

Singh S, Taneja M, Majumdar DK. Biological activities of Ocimum sanctum L. fixed oil--an overview. Indian J Exp Biol. 2007 May; 45(5):403-12.

Singh S, Majumdar DK. Evaluation of antiinflammatory activity of fatty acids of Ocimum sanctum fixed oil. Indian J Exp Biol. 1997 Apr; 35(4):380-3.

Samson J, Sheeladevi R, Ravindran R. Oxidative stress in brain and antioxidant activity of Ocimum sanctum in noise exposure. Neurotoxicology. 2007 May;28(3):679-85.

Joshi H, Parle M. Evaluation of nootropic potential of Ocimum sanctum Linn. in mice. Indian J Exp Biol. 2006 Feb;44(2):133-6.

Mondal S, Mirdha BR, Mahapatra SC. The science behind sacredness of Tulsi (Ocimum sanctum Linn.). Indian J Physiol Pharmacol. 2009 Oct-Dec;53(4):291-306.

Lahon K, Das S. Hepatoprotective activity of Ocimum sanctum alcoholic leaf extract against paracetamol-induced liver damage in Albino rats. Pharmacognosy Res. 2011 Jan;3(1):13-8.

Mondal S, Varma S, Bamola VD, Naik SN, Mirdha BR, Padhi MM, Mehta N, Mahapatra SC. Double-blinded randomized controlled trial for immunomodulatory effects of Tulsi (Ocimum sanctum Linn.) leaf extract on healthy volunteers. J Ethnopharmacol. 2011 Jul 14;136(3):452-6.

Ashwagandha (Withania Somnifera)

Ashwagandha is another great adaptogenic herb. It grows in India and also some African countries like Ethiopia where it still grows wild and organic. Withania has been shown to inhibit inflammatory protein production including TNFα induced NF-kappaB and cyclooxygenase-2 (COX-2) enzyme production. Herbal extracts of Withania have been shown to be nurturing of cartilage, likely by reducing inflammatory load and allowing for new protein synthesis and healing. It can also be a great addition to a neural/cognitive formula to prevent nervous exhaustion. Like Holy Basil, Ashwagandha is a great liver tonic and anti-inflammatory.

I must give a word of caution about Withania somnifera. It's not a caution about safety but rather about quality. Ashwagandha is the Indian name for this plant and it commonly goes by this name. Like Holy Basil, much of the Ashwagandha material grown today is not very "adaptogen" active as it's subjected to huge amounts of fertilizers, pesticides and herbicides to get the yield up. In fact, most Ashwagandha is now harvested in one year when in fact the best material takes between five and seven years to fully develop the bioactives responsible for the best adaptogenic effects.

Remember that these compounds are stress response chemicals the plant makes to adapt to stress in its environment. If you give the plant all these modern chemical "goodies" to make its life easy, in return it will reward you with very little in the way of adaptogenic compounds. The rule of stressing the plants out in the right way so they produce what will benefit humans under stress always applies. In an era of commercialization, and sometimes plain old greed, traditional growing methods are shortened and manipulated. This is a big mistake. The very best material for many adaptogens is organic and wild crafted- left to develop potency after a few years of stress.

Tragically, much of the quality stocks are in very short supply. So beware of most adaptogens on the market for this reason. Question the source, the growing methods, and the independent analysis of the material whenever possible. Otherwise you will be wasting your money on junk.

Mulabagal V, Subbaraju GV, Rao CV, Sivaramakrishna C, Dewitt DL, Holmes D, Sung B, Aggarwal BB, Tsay HS, Nair MG. Withanolide sulfoxide from Aswagandha roots inhibits nuclear transcription factor-kappa-B, cyclooxygenase and tumor cell proliferation. Phytother Res. 2009 Jul;23(7):987-92.

Sumantran VN, Kulkarni A, Boddul S, Chinchwade T, Koppikar SJ, Harsulkar A, Patwardhan B, Chopra A, Wagh UV. Chondroprotective potential of root extracts of Withania somnifera in osteoarthritis. J Biosci. 2007 Mar;32(2):299-307.

Khan S, Malik F, Suri KA, Singh J. Molecular insight into the immune up-regulatory properties of the leaf extract of Ashwagandha and identification of Th1 immunostimulatory chemical entity. Vaccine. 2009 Oct 9; 27(43):6080-7.

Kumar P, Kumar A. Possible neuroprotective effect of Withania somnifera root extract against 3-nitropropionic acid-induced behavioral, biochemical, and mitochondrial dysfunction in an animal model of Huntington's disease. J Med Food. 2009 Jun;12(3):591-600.

Kour K, Pandey A, Suri KA, Satti NK, Gupta KK, Bani S. Restoration of stress-induced altered T cell function and corresponding cytokines patterns by Withanolide A. Int Immunopharmacol. 2009 Sep;9(10):1137-44.

Bhatnagar M, Sharma D, Salvi M. Neuroprotective effects of Withania somnifera dunal.: A possible mechanism. Neurochem Res. 2009 Nov;34(11):1975-83.

Maitra R, Porter MA, Huang S, Gilmour BP. Inhibition of NFkappaB by the natural product Withaferin A in cellular models of Cystic Fibrosis inflammation. J Inflamm (Lond). 2009 May 13; 6:15.

Bhattacharya SK, Muruganandam AV. Adaptogenic activity of Withania somnifera: an experimental study using a rat model of chronic stress. Pharmacol Biochem Behav. 2003 Jun; 75(3):547-55.

Rhodiola Rosea (Golden Root)

For centuries, Rhodiola rosea has been used in the traditional medicine of Russia, Scandinavia, and other countries. Traditional folk medicine used Rhodiola rosea to increase physical endurance, work productivity, longevity, resistance to high altitude sickness, and to treat fatigue, depression, anemia, impotence, gastrointestinal ailments, infections, and nervous system disorders. In mountain villages of Siberia, a bouquet of roots is still given to couples prior to marriage to enhance fertility and assure the birth of healthy children. Chinese emperors sent expeditions to Siberia to bring back the "golden root" for medicinal preparations.

The standardization of Rhodiola rosea root extracts has gone through two distinct phases. Initially, in the 1970s, the compound responsible for its unique pharmacological properties was believed to be salidroside (rhodioloside). Therefore, the first generation of Rhodiola rosea tincture/extracts approved by the Russian Pharmacopoeia Committee was standardized to a minimum of 0.8 percent salidroside content. In the late 1980s, demand for Rhodiola rosea-based phytomedicines dramatically increased. The wild-crafted raw material was over-harvested, resulting in a steady decline in the quality and effectiveness of Rhodiola preparations. Scientific investigation revealed that other species of genus Rhodiola (which also contained salidroside) were being substituted for Rhodiola rosea. Many of these were coming from China.

After more than a decade of research, scientists presented evidence in the mid 80's that the chemical composition of Rhodiola rosea root is, in fact, different from other species of genus Rhodiola. Using newly developed methods of analysis, scientists discovered that Rhodiola rosea root contains three cinnamyl alcohol-vicianosides — rosavin, rosin, and rosarin — that are specific to this species. The term rosavins can be used to include rosavin, rosin, and rosarin.

Rhodiola rosea extracts used in most human clinical studies were standardized to minimum 3 percent rosavins and 0.8-1 percent salidroside because the naturally occurring ratio of these compounds in Rhodiola rosea root is approximately 3:1.

Small doses were shown to increase the bioelectrical activity of the brain. Consequently, the cognitive (thinking, analyzing, evaluating, calculating, and planning) functions of the cerebral cortex and the attention, memory, and learning functions of the prefrontal and frontal cortex are enhanced. As an antioxidant, Rhodiola rosea may help protect the nervous system from oxidative damage by free radicals. Stress interferes with memory functions and, over time, causes deterioration in memory systems.

Positive results found in many student testing studies were based on 300 mg/day or more. In medical treatments, the usual doses are 200-600 mg/day. Rhodiola rosea is shown to increase intellectual capacity (particularly by improving perception and processing of information) to a greater degree than an extract of Eleuthero, another popular Russian adaptogen. Rhodiola rosea may affect emotional tone by influencing neurotransmitter monoamine levels (Norepinephrine, Dopamine, Serotonin) in nerve tracts involved in the regulation of mood, anxiety, and emotion in the amygdala, hippocampus, hypothalamus, and midbrain.

A number of studies have shown that Rhodiola rosea increased physical work capacity and dramatically shortened the recovery time between bouts of high-intensity exercise. These studies included normal individuals exposed to maximal work on a bicycle ergometer as well as Winter Olympic-level cross country skiers and biathletes.

In their early research, Soviet pharmacologists Brekhman and Dardymov surveyed the literature on 189 medicinal plants and identified five (including Rhodiola rosea) that met the three defining criteria for an adaptogen:

- An adaptogen should be innocuous and cause minimal disturbance of the normal physiological functions of an organism;
- The action of an adaptogen should be nonspecific (i.e., it should increase resistance to adverse influences of a wide range of harmful factors of physical, chemical, and biological nature);
- An adaptogen may possess a modulating action irrespective of the direction of the prior stress challenge (i.e., if a body parameter is high, the adaptogen brings it down towards normal; if a parameter is low; the adaptogen brings it up towards normal).

Brown RP, Gerbarg PL, Ramazanov Z. Rhodiola rosea: A Phytomedicinal Overview. HerbalGram. 2002; 56:40-52

Rhodiola rosea has very few if any side effects. Most athletes find that it improves their mood, energy level, and mental clarity. Some individuals, particularly those who tend to be anxious, may feel overly activated, jittery, or agitated. If this occurs, a smaller dose with very gradual increases may be needed. Rhodiola rosea should be taken early in the day because it can interfere with sleep or cause vivid dreams (not nightmares) during the first few weeks. It is contraindicated in overly excited states. Because Rhodiola rosea has an activating antidepressant effect, it should not be used in individuals with bipolar disorder who are vulnerable to becoming manic when given antidepressants or stimulants.

Acute Rhodiola rosea ingestion decreases heart rate response to submaximal exercise and appears to improve endurance exercise performance by decreasing the perception of effort. It is also anxiolytic meaning it reduces anxiety. For athletes who become anxious before competition, Rhodiola rosea may help to normalize excessive anxiousness yet maintain sharpness and focus.

Parisi A, Tranchita E, Duranti G, Ciminelli E, Quaranta F, Ceci R, Cerulli C, Borrione P, Saba-

tini S. Effects of chronic Rhodiola Rosea supplementation on sport performance and antioxidant capacity in trained male: preliminary results. J Sports Med Phys Fitness. 2010 Mar; 50(1):57-63.

Azizov AP, Seĭfulla RD. The effect of elton, leveton, fitoton and adapton on the work capacity of experimental animals. Eksp Klin Farmakol. 1998 May-Jun; 61(3):61-3.

Spasov AA, Mandrikov VB, Mironova IA. The effect of the preparation rodakson on the psychophysiological and physical adaptation of students to an academic load. Eksp Klin Farmakol. 2000 Jan-Feb; 63(1):76-8.

Spasov AA, Wikman GK, Mandrikov VB, Mironova IA, Neumoin VV. A double-blind, placebo-controlled pilot study of the stimulating and adaptogenic effect of Rhodiola rosea SHR-5 extract on the fatigue of students caused by stress during an examination period with a repeated low-dose regimen. Phytomedicine. 2000 Apr; 7(2):85-9.

Shevtsov VA, Zholus BI, Shervarly VI, Vol'skij VB, Korovin YP, Khristich MP, Roslyakova NA, Wikman G. A randomized trial of two different doses of a SHR-5 Rhodiola rosea extract versus placebo and control of capacity for mental work. Phytomedicine. 2003 Mar;10(2-3):95-105.

Bystritsky A, Kerwin L, Feusner JD. A pilot study of Rhodiola rosea (Rhodax) for generalized anxiety disorder (GAD). J Altern Complement Med. 2008 Mar;14(2):175-80.

Noreen EE, Buckley JG, Lewis SL, Brandauer J, Stuempfle KJ. The effects of an acute dose of Rhodiola rosea on endurance exercise performance. J Strength Cond Res. 2013 Mar;27(3):839-47.

*"If you don't know where you are going,
you might wind up someplace else."*
~ Yogi Berra

Eleutherococcus Senticosus
(Eleuthero, Acanthopanax Senticosus, Ciwujia)

The active ingredients of this plant are typically concentrated in the root and mainly consist of chemically distinct glycosides called eleutherosides A-M. In addition to its anti-fatigue and anti-stress effects, the plant also exhibits immunomodulatory effects.

Eleutherococcus affects cytokine expression, inducing and enhancing the actions of IL-1 and IL-6.

Much of the early research with Eleuthero was conducted by Israel Brekhman MD. Dr. Brekhman was in the Department of Problem of Regulation Biological Processes, Pacific Oceanological Institute, Far-East Department of Academy of Sciences of the USSR, in Vladivostok, Russia. Brekhman was a student of Nikolai Lazarev and he took the early adaptogen research of Lazarev to a new level by analyzing thousands of plants for potential adaptogenic qualities.

I first met Dr. Brekhman in 1990 and enjoyed learning about adaptogens from him. He told me a story of studying Eleuthero on rats, where when they used a control group of animals they gave them sugar from a local factory as a placebo. The stressed rats on the placebo actually performed quite well on the sugar, which was surprising to the scientists. They went back to the sugar factory manager and discovered that what they used for the control was a raw sugar rich in molasses, a dark, viscous liquid made from sugar beets. To the surprise of the research group, they discovered that the bioactive substances in the molasses also had adaptogenic effects. Brekhman eventually formulated dietary supplements containing a number of adaptogenic herbs plus molasses.

There have been a number of research studies conducted on animals, average individuals, and athletes showing that Eleuthero increases work performance, total work, and time to exhaustion. Like many adaptogens, Eleuthero also has anti-inflammatory, neuroprotective, and cognitive enhancing qualities. Many Russian studies were investigated in human trials including truck drivers, factory workers, students, and sportsmen. You can still find tinctures of Eleuthero in any Apteka (pharmacy) in Russia.

Lee D, Park J, Yoon J, Kim MY, Choi HY, Kim H. Neuroprotective effects of Eleutherococcus senticosus bark on transient global cerebral ischemia in rats. J Ethnopharmacol. 2012 Jan 6;139(1):6-11.

Huang LZ, Wei L, Zhao HF, Huang BK, Rahman K, Qin LP. The effect of Eleutheroside E on behavioral alterations in murine sleep deprivation stress model. Eur J Pharmacol. 2011 May 11;658(2-3):150-5.

Bai Y, Tohda C, Zhu S, Hattori M, Komatsu K. Active components from Siberian ginseng (Eleutherococcus senticosus) for protection of amyloid β(25-35)-induced neuritic atrophy in cultured rat cortical neurons. J Nat Med. 2011 Jul;65(3-4):417-23.

Kuo J, Chen KW, Cheng IS, Tsai PH, Lu YJ, Lee NY. The effect of eight weeks of supplementation with Eleutherococcus senticosus on endurance capacity and metabolism in human. Chin J Physiol. 2010 Apr 30;53(2):105-11.

Tohda C, Ichimura M, Bai Y, Tanaka K, Zhu S, Komatsu K. Inhibitory effects of Eleutherococcus senticosus extracts on amyloid beta(25-35)-induced neuritic atrophy and synaptic loss. J Pharmacol Sci. 2008 Jul;107(3):329-39.

Glatthaar-Saalmüller B, Sacher F, Esperester A. Antiviral activity of an extract derived from roots of Eleutherococcus senticosus. Antiviral Res. 2001 Jun;50(3):223-8.

Asano K, Takahashi T, Miyashita M, Matsuzaka A, Muramatsu S, Kuboyama M, Kugo H, Imai J. Effect of Eleutherococcus senticosus extract on human physical working capacity. Planta Med. 1986 Jun;(3):175-7.

Ahn J, Um MY, Lee H, Jung CH, Heo SH, Ha TY. Eleutheroside E, An Active Component of Eleutherococcus senticosus, Ameliorates Insulin Resistance in Type 2 Diabetic db/db Mice. Evid Based Complement Alternat Med. 2013;2013:934183. Epub 2013 Apr 10.

Bespalov VG, Aleksandrov VA, Iaremenko KV, Davydov VV, Lazareva NL, Limarenko AIu, Slepian LI, Petrov AS, Troian DN. The inhibiting effect of phytoadaptogenic preparations from bioginseng, Eleutherococcus senticosus and Rhaponticum carthamoides on the development of nervous system tumors in rats induced by N-nitrosoethylurea. Vopr Onkol. 1992;38(9):1073-80.

"I firmly believe that any man's finest hour, the greatest fulfillment of all that he holds dear, is that moment when he has worked his heart out in a good cause and lies exhausted on the field of battle - victorious."
~ Vince Lombardi

Leuzea Carthamoides (Rhaponticum, Maral Root)

I wrote about Leuzea earlier because it's a strategic material in the Russian pharma program for its high concentration of 20-hydroxyecdysone which increases RNA protein translation and protein synthesis. While the purified extract of Leuzea is used in Russian pharmacopeia and can also be found in an Apteka, over the years of working with the material I've come to love a less refined crude extract because it's rich in various other beneficial phytosterols and other bioactives including phenolics (flavonoids and phenolic acids) polyacetylenes, sesquiterpene lactones, triterpenoid glycosides and terpenes. Crude Leuzea extracts exhibit diverse biological effects such as antioxidant, immunomodulatory, anticancerogenic, antimicrobial, antiparasitic and insect repellent actions. The total daily dose of crude Leuzea carthamoides is around 300 milligrams.

Summary

There are many adaptogens to choose from which you can introduce into your training plan. I recommend adaptogenic extracts from plants more than I do from animal sources such as non-ossified deer or caribou (reindeer) antler. Most antler serum is of poor quality today and the good stuff is super expensive. In contrast, plant based adaptogens are of relatively good quality if purchased from well-established suppliers. I prefer organic material but sometimes this is not available. As long as the manufacturer is testing the extract material for a standard bioactive it is probably of good quality. Trouble is many manufacturers today simply go by what their raw material supplier tells them. But certificate of analysis sheets are often falsified, especially for Chinese material. I prefer to purchase materials from Germany and Italy because their bioactive quality and purity standards are high. For other countries we analyze materials consistently and do not take the word of the supplier. This is not common in the industry but it must be done, otherwise you're guessing as to quality.

I mentioned a few of the many adaptogens and there are certainly many more including Panax ginseng (Korean and Chinese), Panax quinquefolius (American ginseng), Pfaffia paniculata (Suma or Brazilian ginseng), moomyo (Asphaltum, Shilajit), Spirulina platensis, Schisandra chinensis, Lycium barbarum (Wolfberry or Goji Berry) and Asparagus racemosus. Doses of all adaptogens will vary depending upon how concentrated the material is, from raw material to a highly extracted concentrate. If the extract is lightly extracted, such as a 5:1 or 10:1 the dose should be around 100 milligrams to 300mg. It is best to consume quality material on the lighter side as all adaptogens I know of are hormetic and a little goes a long way to improving performance, while a lot can be toxic.

Alexander Karelin dominated Greco-Roman wrestling, winning three consecutive Olympic Gold medals (Seoul, Barcelona, and Atlanta) before settling for Silver in Sydney after being upset by American Rulon Gardner in the finals. Brunner Photo.

NEUROLOGIC ERGOGENIC NUTRIENTS

This is a very important chapter of the book as it explores new science that athletes aren't leveraging, but should. When you better understand the link between the nervous system and skeletal muscles you will be primed to achieve extra gains in explosiveness and athleticism.

Athleticism in explosive sports is not simply big muscle. If it were, sprinters, tennis players, weight throwers, football players, and the like would be bodybuilders. Likewise, bodybuilders would be running the 100 meters in the Olympics, pass routes in the NFL, and shooting three-pointers in the NCAA® Final Four. Yet many athletes equate bigger muscles with better performance. This is true only if the muscle is functional and this functionality requires crosstalk between many parts of the nervous system and the muscle system. When we're talking nerve meets muscle for explosiveness we're talking motor units.

Motor unit recruitment is the progressive activation of a muscle by successive recruitment of contractile units (motor units) to accomplish increasing gradations of contractile strength. A motor unit consists of one motor neuron and all of the muscle fibers it innervates. All muscles consist of a number of motor units. The fibers belonging to a motor unit are dispersed and intermingle amongst fibers of other units. The muscle fibers belonging to one motor unit can be spread throughout part, or most of the entire muscle, depending on the number of fibers and size of the muscle. When a motor neuron is activated, all of the muscle fibers innervated by the motor neuron are stimulated and they contract. The activation of one motor neuron will result in a weak but distributed muscle contraction. The activation of more motor neurons will result in more muscle fibers being activated, and therefore a stronger muscle contraction.

Motor unit recruitment is a measure of how many motor neurons are activated in a particular muscle, and therefore is a measure of how many muscle fibers of that muscle are activated. The higher the recruitment the stronger the muscle contraction will be. Motor units are generally recruited in order of smallest to largest (smallest motoneurons to largest motoneurons, from slow to fast twitch as contraction increases. The speed at which motor units engage muscle fibers is what separates the men from the boys.

Explosiveness is important in many sports. In addition to the increase in motor-unit firing frequency contributing to the increase in force development, the synchronized activation of motor units during heavy resistance training contributes to the athlete's ability to produce rapid high-power output which is the key to sports performance. Adaptive alterations can be induced in the neuromuscular system in response to specific types of training. These adaptations, pertinent to many explosive sports, includes improvement in traits such as visual acuity, hearing, reaction time, starting power, maximal velocity, striking force, and power-endurance.

In speed training, it's important to build as many fast motor units as possible, which are more suitable for fast movements. The gains in sprint performance occur in both the initial acceleration as well as speed-maintenance phases. The ability to better accelerate quickly from a stationary position will provide a competitive advantage for athletes. Muscles convert metabolic energy into mechanical work, allowing for contraction to occur. Nutritionally, research has shown specific nutrients can be used to both nurture the motor units and also help to conduct the electrical impulse from nerve to muscle. This is a missing link in most all athletic training programs. Coaches and athletes alike excessively focus their attention on nutrition ergogenics to build muscle (like a bodybuilder) rather than address the neuromuscular explosiveness aspect. Yet this is an area where great improvements in explosiveness can be made.

Post-activation potentiation (PAP) is induced by a voluntary conditioning contraction (CC), performed typically at a maximal or near-maximal intensity, and has consistently been shown to increase both peak force and rate of force development during subsequent twitch contractions. However, the CC might also induce fatigue, and it is the balance between PAP and fatigue that will determine the net effect on performance of a subsequent explosive activity. Most sports not only require an explosive effort one time, but multiple times. The PAP-fatigue relationship is affected by several variables including contraction volume and intensity, recovery period following the contraction, type of contraction, type of subsequent activity, subject characteristics, and the metabolic milieu found in the motor unit muscle synergy (nutrients that allow for strong contractions to occur).

Most science shows that for lengthening contractions of a wide range of efforts and speeds, fast-twitch muscle fibers cannot be selectively recruited without activity of the slow-twitch fibers of the same muscle. Both fibers must be developed and nourished in conjunction with their respective motor unit. So the question we should ask is what can we do nutritionally to enhance both the training as well as the competitive efforts?

I'm going to introduce some rarely promoted nutrients that pretty much fall under the strength building radar. Perhaps this is because they are not as sexy as muscle building nutrition like protein powders, or endurance nutrition like hydration/electrolyte drinks. I think it's also because the majority of wannabe athletes, muscle heads, and couch warriors are just not interested in making their muscles perform with incredible explosiveness, so to crush their competition. That's why glorified belly wash electrolyte drinks, nutrition (candy) bars, sugar packed gels, and mega-multi ingredient flavored powder drink mixes are so popular with the masses.

To specifically stimulate the strongest most powerful contractions, in the minimal amount of time, often for several efforts, you just cannot afford to focus your attention on sissy nutrition products. You must feed your entire motor unit-muscle system.

The Neuromuscular Junction and Explosiveness

I've written a bunch on motor units, but to really get to how these link-up with muscle fibers we need to discuss the neuromuscular junction. The neuromuscular junction connects the nervous system to the muscular system via synapses between efferent nerve fibers and muscle fibers. In simple terms, the neuron (nerve) from a motor unit which is charged to innervate a muscle fiber never actually touches the fiber.

Nerve impulses, also known as action potentials, travel from the brain or spinal cord to trigger the contraction of skeletal muscles. An action potential travels down a motor neuron to a skeletal muscle fiber. The site where the motor neuron excites a skeletal muscle fiber is the neuromuscular junction. This junction is the point of contact between the axon terminals of a motor neuron and the motor end plate of the skeletal muscle fiber.

There are seven coordinated steps necessary for a muscle contraction to occur and nutrition plays a role in the entire process which includes calcium ion diffusion, the release, diffusion and binding of acetylcholine (ACh) to ACh receptors on muscle fibers, sodium entry and potassium exit from the muscle fiber, reaching an action potential (to initiate a contraction), and cessation of contractions when ACh diffuses from the synapse or is degraded by the degrading enzyme acetylcholinesterase. So you can see that acetylcholine, which is made up of acetic acid and choline, is a major player in transmitting the nerve impulse to the muscle fiber to cause a contraction. No acetylcholine, no contraction. Likewise, plenty of acetylcholine in the synapse gives the athlete strong muscle contractions.

Klaver-Król EG, Henriquez NR, Oosterloo SJ, Klaver P, Kuipers H, Zwarts MJ. Distribution of motor unit potential velocities in the biceps brachii muscle of sprinters and endurance athletes during prolonged dynamic exercises at low force levels. J Electromyogr Kinesiol. 2010 Dec;20(6):1115-24.

Tillin NA, Bishop D. Factors modulating post-activation potentiation and its effect on performance of subsequent explosive activities. Sports Med. 2009;39(2):147-66.

Acetylcholine is not only important in firing muscle fibers but is also essential for efficient brain function. ACh has functions both in the peripheral nervous system (PNS) and in the central nervous system (CNS) as a neuromodulator. ACh is released from one neuron and binds with another neuron and can improve learning, shorten reaction time, maximize striking force, and increase speed traits. In other words, you need lots of acetylcholine to be explosive. Another really interesting finding is that ACh is not just replenished in the synapse but can also be replenished via the circulation from the periphery.

Chiou-Tan FY, Chiou GC. Contribution of circulating acetylcholine to sensory nerve conduction augmentation. Life Sci. 2000;66(16):1509-18.

Reducing Acetylcholinesterase for Timely Powerful Muscle Contractions

Now for the really juicy and practical stuff: How to raise your acetylcholine levels and innervation potentials so you have plenty of this neurotransmitter when you want it to make your muscle fibers fire at will- for maximum explosiveness. This requires certain nutrients to either replenish ACh stores by supplying raw materials for re-synthesis, or to reduce the acetylcholinesterase enzyme activity to maintain ACh in the junction longer. I have years of experience and practical suggestions for both.

If you want ACh to remain in the neuromuscular junction longer to potentiate contractions and also in the neural junctions to enhance cognition and reaction, a good way is to slightly inhibit the acetylcholinesterase (AChE) enzyme that is breaking down ACh into acetic acid and choline. You need a natural acetylcholinesterase inhibitor or AChEI.

There are pharmaceuticals that are AChEI's such as Physostigmine, Donepezil, and Tacrine, as well as proven plant based compounds such as Galanthamine and Huperzine A/B.

Galanthamine

Galanthamine, an alkaloid derivative isolated from snowdrop (Galanthus nivalis L.), is an effective anticholinesterase compound which has shown promise in improving reaction time, starting power, and repetitive striking force exercises. I first formulated with Galanthamine back in 2002 and found it to be most effective as it reduces AChE by about 50%. The daily dose for galanthamine is between 15mg and 20mg. More of this compound is not better and likely toxic. I was working with 90% pure galanthamine in the lab one day and had a beaker with some residual material at the bottom, so I did as any nutty scientist would do (well, maybe the nuttiest of scientists) and added some water, swirled it around and then downed the alkaloid. In just a few minutes I experienced profuse sweating, my heart was racing, and I had to sit down before I passed out- which taught me two things: 1) be careful with dose, as more is not always better; and 2) don't be a human guinea pig when you really don't know the dose.

Huperzine A/B

Huperzine A (Hup-A) is a lycopodium alkaloid from the club moss Huperzia serrata, which has been used as a therapeutic agent in several neurological disorders. Hup-A is effective for individuals who have cognitive decline. It is a very good AChEI.

Recently a novel role of Hup-A in neurogenesis (growth of nerve cells) was discovered which provides a new insight into its therapeutic effects in neurological disorders via a neurogenesis-related mechanism. HUP-A may also provide safe and effective management for chronic postneurotrauma pain by reestablishing homeostasis of sensory circuits.

I've used Hup-A in synergistic formulas with many college age explosive athletes, professional athletes, and even masters athletes with good results. The dose I generally use is between 100 micrograms (mcg) to 200 mcg daily. Micrograms are 1/1000th of a milligram, so we're talking .1-.2 milligrams which is not much. Like galanthamine, you don't need to take more as it is likely too strong in excess.

Years ago we did a study with college age baseball players. It was a double blind placebo crossover study where we gave one group of 10 the formula with Hup-A and the other group a placebo capsule. The athletes trained for 10 days and were measured for reaction and quickness as well as observational data from the coaches. After a 10 day washout we flipped the groups and repeated a 10 day cycle. In both cases the athletes using the supplement with Hup-A performed much better than the placebo group on all measurements of explosiveness, especially reaction and striking power. In addition, the coaches, who did not know which athletes were using the Hup-A supplement, rated the Hup-A users higher in performance 100%.

I've also found Hup-A to be useful for masters athletes, especially in sports older athletes compete in such as golf, tennis, and even billiards. The improvements in "touch" or fine motor skills are often quite dramatic.

Mohamed T, Osman W, Tin G, Rao PP. Selective inhibition of human acetylcholinesterase by xanthine derivatives: in vitro inhibition and molecular modeling investigations. Bioorg Med Chem Lett. 2013 Aug 1; 23(15):4336-41.

Pohanka M, Dobes P. Caffeine inhibits acetylcholinesterase, but not butyrylcholinesterase. Int J Mol Sci. 2013 May 8; 14(5):9873-82.

Okello EJ, Leylabi R, McDougall GJ. Inhibition of acetylcholinesterase by green and white tea and their simulated intestinal metabolites. Food Funct. 2012 Jun; 3(6):651-61.

Song HR, Woo YS, Wang HR, Jun TY, Bahk WM. Effect of the timing of acetylcholinesterase inhibitor ingestion on sleep. Int Clin Psychopharmacol. 2013 Nov; 28(6):346-8.

Radicheva N, Vydevska M, Mileva K. Nivalin P-induced changes in muscle fiber membrane processes. Methods Find Exp Clin Pharmacol. 1996 Jun; 18(5):301-8.

Krivoĭ II, Seĭ TP. Postsynaptic potentiation of end plate currents in the rat diaphragm at different levels of synaptic acetylcholinesterase activity. Biull Eksp Biol Med. 1991 May; 111(5):458-60.

Ma T, Gong K, Yan Y, Zhang L, Tang P, Zhang X, Gong Y. Huperzine A promotes hippocampal neurogenesis in vitro and in vivo. Brain Res. 2013 Apr 19;1506:35-43.

Yu D, Thakor DK, Han I, Ropper AE, Haragopal H, Sidman RL, Zafonte R, Schachter SC, Teng YD. Alleviation of chronic pain following rat spinal cord compression injury with multimodal actions of huperzine A. Proc Natl Acad Sci U S A. 2013 Feb 19;110(8):E746-55. 5.

Ruan Q, Liu F, Gao Z, Kong D, Hu X, Shi D, Bao Z, Yu Z. The anti-inflamm-aging and hepatoprotective effects of huperzine A in D-galactose-treated rats. Mech Ageing Dev. 2013 Mar;134(3-4):89-97.

Yang L, Ye CY, Huang XT, Tang XC, Zhang HY. Decreased accumulation of subcellular amyloid-β with improved mitochondrial function mediates the neuroprotective effect of huperzine A. J Alzheimers Dis. 2012;31(1):131-42.

Xu ZQ, Liang XM, Juan-Wu, Zhang YF, Zhu CX, Jiang XJ. Treatment with Huperzine A improves cognition in vascular dementia patients. Cell Biochem Biophys. 2012 Jan;62(1):55-8.

Citicoline (CDP-Choline)

Choline participates in several relevant neurochemical processes. It is the precursor and metabolite of acetylcholine (ACh) and plays a role in single-carbon metabolism and is an essential component of different membrane phospholipids (PLs). PLs are structural components of cell membranes involved in intraneuronal signal transduction. In a practical sense this can mean that muscle cells can communicate more efficiently with nerve cells.

There have been many studies done using choline and choline-containing phospholipids such as lecithin, but the results have not been good. Supplements containing choline or lecithin are pretty much a waste of time if your goal is to refuel the acetylcholine level at the neuromuscular junction for improved explosiveness.

One useful nutritional is Citicoline. Cytidine 5'-diphosphocholine (CDP-choline or citicoline) is a highly bioavailable compound with potential benefits for aiding neural repair and increasing acetylcholine levels in the central and peripheral nervous system. Many researchers have investigated the use of CDP-choline for various types of neurological insult or conditions, including stroke, traumatic brain injury, and Alzheimer disease.

The only downside to citicoline may be the dose and price. The human dose extrapolated from rat studies falls between 16mg/kg to a high 52mg/kg. For an athlete weighing 180 pounds, the daily low dose would be 1.3 grams, and for an athlete weighing 220 pounds it would be 1.6 grams.

Tayebati SK, Amenta F. Choline-containing phospholipids: relevance to brain functional pathways. Clin Chem Lab Med. 2013 Mar 1;51(3):513-21.

Arenth PM, Russell KC, Ricker JH, Zafonte RD. CDP-choline as a biological supplement during neurorecovery: a focused review. PM R. 2011 Jun;3(6 Suppl 1):S123-31.

Conant R, Schauss AG. Therapeutic applications of citicoline for stroke and cognitive dysfunction in the elderly: a review of the literature. Altern Med Rev. 2004 Mar;9(1):17-31.

α-GPC (L-alpha-glycerylphosphorylcholine, choline alfoscerate)

α-GPC is another acetylcholine precursor that has been on the market for several years now as AlphaSize® by Chemi Nutra and is just now taking hold with athletes. I really like this ergogenic nutrient. Early research with AlphaSize® α-GPC showed it increases ACh quite efficiently and more so than other precursors, including citicoline.

Several studies coming out of Russia the past few years show that α-GPC is a potent neuroprotective agent. This is an advantage for explosive athletes for two key reasons. First, α-GPC can protect the health and function of the neuromuscular junction from excessive stress and inflammation during intense training. Second, while not yet confirmed, it is likely that α-GPC will be of benefit after head trauma in contact sports as it shows neuroprotective and anti-inflammatory actions.

One final benefit to α-GPC may be its potential to increase growth hormone. In a recent study eight young men with an average age of 25 years consumed 1,000mg of α-GPC. Plasma GH increased significantly 60 minutes after α-GPC consumption and liver fat oxidation increased as well.

Dosage suggestions:

I recommend 400mg of AlphaSize® α-GPC three times daily (1,200 mg/day) for high school and college age athletes. From experience with elite and professional athletes I find they respond best to 2,000mg to 2,400 milligrams daily. α-GPC works extremely well stacked with Huperzine A- 100mcg's for high school age and 200mcg's for college and professional explosive athletes. Use this stack mainly during competitions for excellent results.

Brownawell AM, Carmines EL, Montesano F. Safety assessment of AGPC as a food ingredient. Food Chem Toxicol. 2011 Jun; 49(6):1303-15.

De Jesus Moreno Moreno M. Cognitive improvement in mild to moderate Alzheimer's dementia after treatment with the acetylcholine precursor choline alfoscerate: a multicenter, double-blind, randomized, placebo-controlled trial. Clin Ther. 2003 Jan; 25(1):178-93.

Amenta F, Tayebati SK, Vitali D, Di Tullio MA. Association with the cholinergic precursor choline alphoscerate and the cholinesterase inhibitor rivastigmine: an approach for enhancing cholinergic neurotransmission. Mech Ageing Dev. 2006 Feb; 127(2):173-9.

Antal A, Kéri S, Bodis-Wollner I. L-alpha-glycerylphosphorylcholine enhances the amplitude of the pattern electroretinogram in rhesus monkeys. A pilot study. Neurobiology (Bp). 1999; 7(4):407-12.

Sigala S, Imperato A, Rizzonelli P, Casolini P, Missale C, Spano P. L-alpha-glycerylphosphorylcholine antagonizes scopolamine-induced amnesia and enhances hippocampal cholinergic transmission in the rat. Eur J Pharmacol. 1992 Feb 18; 211(3):351-8.

Kostenko EV, Petrova LV, Artemova Ilu, Vdovichenko TV, Ganzhula PA, Ismailov AM, Lisenker LN, Petrov SV, Otcheskaia OV, Rotor LD, Khozova AA, Boĭko AN. The use of cerepro (choline alfoscerate) in the treatment of outpatients with chronic progressive cerebrovascular disease. Zh Nevrol Psikhiatr Im S S Korsakova. 2012; 112(3 Pt 1):24-30.

Suchy J, Chan A, Shea TB. Dietary supplementation with a combination of alpha-lipoic acid, acetyl-L-carnitine, glycerophosphocoline, docosahexaenoic acid, and phosphatidylserine reduces oxidative damage to murine brain and improves cognitive performance. Nutr Res. 2009 Jan; 29(1):70-4.

Onishchenko LS, Gaikova ON, Yanishevskii SN. Changes at the focus of experimental ischemic stroke treated with neuroprotective agents. Neurosci Behav Physiol. 2008 Jan; 38(1):49-54.

Tomassoni D, Avola R, Mignini F, Parnetti L, Amenta F. Effect of treatment with choline alphoscerate on hippocampus microanatomy and glial reaction in spontaneously hypertensive rats. Brain Res. 2006 Nov 20; 1120(1):183-90.

Tőkés T, Varga G, Garab D, Nagy Z, Fekete G, Tuboly E, Plangár I, Mán I, Szabó RE, Szabó

Z, Volford G, Ghyczy M, Kaszaki J, Boros M, Hideghéty K. Peripheral inflammatory activation after hippocampus irradiation in the rat. Int J Radiat Biol. 2013 Sep 13. [Epub ahead of print]

Kawamura T, Okubo T, Sato K, Fujita S, Goto K, Hamaoka T, Iemitsu M. Glycerophosphocholine enhances growth hormone secretion and fat oxidation in young adults. Nutrition. 2012 Nov-Dec; 28(11-12):1122-6.

Bacopa monnieri

Bacopa monnieri is a commonly used Ayurvedic herb for mental disorders. The standardized extract has significant anti-oxidant effect, anxiolytic (anxiousness) activity, cholinergic potentiation, and improves memory retention. Bacopa may also be a good addition to a cognitive cocktail consisting of α-GPC, Hup-A, and Bacopa extract.

Anand T, Phani Kumar G, Pandareesh MD, Swamy MS, Khanum F, Bawa AS. Effect of bacoside extract from Bacopa monniera on physical fatigue induced by forced swimming. Phytother Res. 2012 Apr;26(4):587-93.

Shinomol GK, Raghunath N, Bharath MM, Muralidhara. Prophylaxis with Bacopa monnieri attenuates acrylamide induced neurotoxicity and oxidative damage via elevated antioxidant function. Cent Nerv Syst Agents Med Chem. 2013 Mar;13(1):3-12.

Saraf MK, Prabhakar S, Anand A. Neuroprotective effect of Bacopa monniera on ischemia induced brain injury. Pharmacol Biochem Behav. 2010 Dec;97(2):192-7.

Saraf MK, Anand A, Prabhakar S. Scopolamine induced amnesia is reversed by Bacopa monniera through participation of kinase-CREB pathway. Neurochem Res. 2010 Feb;35(2):279-87.

Vitamin B6 (P-5-P) and B12 (Methylcobalamin)

I'm careful not to use many vitamins within the training plans of explosive athletes because some cause more problems than they yield benefits. Vitamins B6 and B12 are an exception.

Vitamin B6 is one of the best natural compounds around to correct all kinds of nerve dysfunction. But B6 is not always easy to get through the diet. Cooking, freezing, canning, storing or processing foods can deplete their vitamin B6 content by as much as 50%? And some people, especially older persons, cannot use certain forms of vitamin B6 like pyridoxine effectively. P-5-P is the active coenzyme form of B6 and it's of great benefit to athletes.

B6 in the form of Pyridoxal-5-Phosphate (P-5-P) can help with fuel storage and ATP utilization by improving fat oxidation during exercise and in recovery. P5P plays a fundamental role in amino acid metabolism, heme biosynthesis, neurotransmitter biosynthesis, collagen formation, glucocorticoid activity, and helps to balance your sodium and potassium levels by regulating the electrical functioning of your nerves, heart and musculoskeletal system. Enzymes dependent on PLP focus a wide variety of chemical reactions mainly involving amino acids. Balanced sodium and potassium levels are essential for strong muscle contractions. Recommended dose for athletes is 20 to 30mg of B6 as P5P daily.

Methylcobalamin is the most potent form of Vitamin B12 found in nature. We need methylcobalamin for the healthy development and function of our circulatory, immune and nervous systems. Methylcobalamin is the only active form of Vitamin B-12 in the brain outside the mitochondria. The liver must convert cyanocobalamin, another form of B12, to methylcobalamin in order for the vitamin to do its biochemical work in the brain. When the complex conversion of cyanocobalamin is not completed, the brain is robbed of the benefits of methylcobalamin.

Methylcobalamin increases the Erk1/2 and AKT activities which amplify the mTORC1 pathway leading to skeletal muscle growth. When the nervous system is under extreme stress such as heavy training loads or long competitive seasons methylcobalamin will likely help restore axon and neuron function for strong muscle contractions.

Zemel MB, Bruckbauer A. Effects of a leucine and pyridoxine-containing nutraceutical on fat oxidation, and oxidative and inflammatory stress in overweight and obese subjects. Nutrients. 2012 Jun; 4(6):529-41.

Chiang EP, Smith DE, Selhub J, Dallal G, Wang YC, Roubenoff R. Inflammation causes tissue-specific depletion of vitamin B6. Arthritis Res Ther. 2005; 7(6):R1254-62.

Livanova NB, Chebotareva NA, Eronina TB, Kurganov BI. Pyridoxal 5'-phosphate as a catalytic and conformational cofactor of muscle glycogen phosphorylase B. Biochemistry (Mosc). 2002 Oct; 67(10):1089-98.

Hemendinger RA, Armstrong EJ 3rd, Brooks BR. Methyl Vitamin B12 but not methylfolate rescues a motor neuron-like cell line from homocysteine-mediated cell death. Toxicol Appl Pharmacol. 2011 Mar 15; 251(3):217-25.

Mikhaĭlov VV, Mikhaĭlov VV, Avakumov VM. Mechanism of the effect of methylcobalamin on the recovery of neuromuscular functions in mechanical and toxin denervation. Farmakol Toksikol. 1983 Nov-Dec;46(6):9-12.

CONCUSSION

Athletes today are more aware of the association of mild traumatic brain injuries, also known as concussion, with long-term cognitive deficits related to trauma-induced neurodegeneration. Research has shown that concussions in young athletes require longer recovery. Athletes at any age who experience multiple concussions are especially vulnerable to another concussion.

I formulated my first post-concussion nutritional several years ago. One NFL player I worked with experienced a couple bad concussions in his rookie season and I knew that this couldn't be good. So I began to research concussions and also some potential nutritionals to prevent post-concussion damage. Blunt force traumas like concussions trigger prolonged post-trauma events such as oxidative stress, inflammation, infiltration of inflammatory and other cells, acidification, excitotoxicity, ischemia, and the loss of calcium homeostasis, all of which cause neurotoxicity and neuron death. Post-concussion symptoms are often headache, dizziness, fatigue, and personality changes.

There is currently no Food and Drug Administration–approved pharmacological intervention to treat concussion, but many have been attempted with generally limited success. These treatments include corticosteroids, free radical scavengers and antioxidants, drugs to inhibit arachidonic acid inflammatory response, and drugs that modify monamine function.

Because there are a number of nutrients which are shown in the science to reduce inflammation under various health conditions, several may be potentially useful to athletes, both as a preventive and as a treatment. Of course the first thing an athlete should do is to take time away from their sport and to eliminate any cognitive stress such as computer work, excessive studying, etc.

It's a tough thing to ask athletes to take time off from training and competition. They may be reluctant to do so because they don't want to let down their team, but for their long-term health and future performance it's vital to rest the brain and also take in healthy nutrients that will restore brain health by reducing excessive inflammation and reset neurological channels. Athletes can also consume a healthy diet and specific nutrients pre-concussion as a preventive or trauma reducer which may dampen the effects of the concussion and help them get back faster.

Because the "watchful-waiting" treatment currently advocated for those with Post-Concussion Syndrome (PCS) is not a treatment and does not address the underlying organ involved, the brain, there are many who advocate alternative methods to address brain healing and recovery after concussion.

The brain itself is made up mostly of fatty acids; the most predominant, making up 40% of these fatty acids, is the Omega-3 fatty acid docosahexaenoic acid (DHA). DHA can be obtained from fatty fish like salmon and tuna, fish oil supplements, or from microalgae grown commercially in large vats. Omega-3s are called EFAs because our body cannot produce them and must extract them from the food we eat. a-Linolenic acid (ALA) is also an important part of the omega-3 EFAs because it, along with DHA and EPA, is used as a structural component in every organ of the body. Walnuts, flax seeds, and chia seeds have lots of ALA. Besides being part of the bilipid membrane in every cell of our body, in the brain, they enhance neuronal cell fluidity and stability and act as part of the neurotransmitter system. Omega-3s have been found to have significant health benefits in disease prevention and treatment, especially for the brain. Their major benefits in this area are as both an essential cellular component and, once converted, anti-inflammatory prostaglandins. By countering inflammation, the adequate consumption of omega-3 EFAs can help to decrease the production of inflammatory prostaglandins and potentially decrease brain trauma–related inflammation. I covered Omega-3s earlier and want to reiterate that Omega-3s have a positive influence on muscle protein synthesis and neuromuscular activities (reaction, starting power, fine motor skills, etc.).

Researchers have shown that consumption of EPA has a favorable effect on blood flow and metabolism in the brains of rats suffering from brain cell death caused by an interruption in blood flow. In other studies, omega-3 EFAs were shown to decrease the toxic effects of glutamate, which is released in large amounts after traumatic brain injury and can lead to the death of still-surviving brain cells within the area of the injury. Additionally, omega-3 EFAs have been found to stabilize cell membranes by inhibiting the release of arachidonic acid, a polyunsaturated omega-6 fatty acid that increases inflammatory proteins which cause tissue destruction when produced in excess.

Ricks Brain Trauma Prevention and Restorative Cocktail

Over the years I've improved on the formula that I recommend to athletes in explosive sports and who are prone to brain trauma. The definition of post-concussion is a little loose and can mean short term loss of consciousness, short-term memory loss, a bad headache, and the like from a blow to the head. What the formula is designed to do is to dial down the inflammatory and free radical load on the brain, to reset cell energetics, and improve healthy blood flow.

Did I do a double blind, placebo controlled, crossover study on dozens of athletes? I did not. I didn't even conduct a controlled test on animals, although I did use an earlier formula on my chocolate lab Sam who suffered a spinal (fibrocartilaginous) embolism, a stroke-like event of the spinal cord, which caused immediate paralysis of Sams hind legs.

A spinal embolism is when disk materials between the bones of the spine detach and lodge in nearby blood vessels. Recovery usually takes a long time and many dogs never recover. My dog happened to have a very severe form and I was advised by my veterinarian to put Sam down. Sam was a great dog and the male dog in my breeding pair- he sired forty puppies. So I gave Sam my brain trauma cocktail and the end result was that he recovered amazingly well, getting full use of his hind legs back, and siring another ten puppies before we retired him from breeding. Certainly this is not definitive scientifically but I know Sam could not have recovered without the cocktail, and especially in such a short time.

As for athletes, I've made nutrient recommendations on many occasions and while the outcomes were good I admit I did not do a true scientific study which would be very hard to do anyway.

Here's my preventive list I recommend for football and soccer players, wrestlers, and others who are prone to head trauma:

- Fish oil EPA/DHA in a combined dose of 1,000 to 2,000mgs daily in both your training and competitive periods.
- Acetyl-L-Carnitine, 500mgs for 1 to 2x in 24 hours with last dose 2 hours before competition, and 500mgs/day for 2-3 days after.
- Vinpocetine, 10-30 mgs daily.

Here is a list of nutrients to take post-trauma to the brain. Some nutrients are primarily focused on increasing the Nrf2 pathway which boosts very potent cytoprotective antioxidant/detox enzymes that also have an influence on inflammation.

Both RONS and inflammation play a sizable role in brain trauma and memory dysfunction so they are addressed with this post-trauma cocktail:

- Lipoic acid, 300mgs twice daily
- Melatonin, 1mg about 30 minutes before bed
- Mixed Tocopherols (Vitamin E), 400iu for a week post-trauma
- Resveratrol, 20mg with 7 mgs of Bioperine® (Piperine from black pepper to enhance absorption) twice daily

- Green Tea, 400mgs (50% EGCG preferred) twice daily.

Palacios HH, Yendluri BB, Parvathaneni K, Shadlinski VB, Obrenovich ME, Leszek J, Gokhman D, Gąsiorowski K, Bragin V, Aliev G. Mitochondrion-specific antioxidants as drug treatments for Alzheimer disease. CNS Neurol Disord Drug Targets. 2011 Mar;10(2):149-62.

Rump TJ, Abdul Muneer PM, Szlachetka AM, Lamb A, Haorei C, Alikunju S, Xiong H, Keblesh J, Liu J, Zimmerman MC, Jones J, Donohue TM Jr, Persidsky Y, Haorah J. Acetyl-L-carnitine protects neuronal function from alcohol-induced oxidative damage in the brain. Free Radic Biol Med. 2010 Nov 30; 49(10):1494-504.

Calabrese V, Giuffrida Stella AM, Calvani M, Butterfield DA. Acetylcarnitine and cellular stress response: roles in nutritional redox homeostasis and regulation of longevity genes. J Nutr Biochem. 2006 Feb; 17(2):73-88.

Calabrese V, Ravagna A, Colombrita C, Scapagnini G, Guagliano E, Calvani M, Butterfield DA, Giuffrida Stella AM. Acetylcarnitine induces heme oxygenase in rat astrocytes and protects against oxidative stress: involvement of the transcription factor Nrf2. J Neurosci Res. 2005 Feb 15; 79(4):509-21.

Sharman EH, Vaziri ND, Ni Z, Sharman KG, Bondy SC. Reversal of biochemical and behavioral parameters of brain aging by melatonin and acetyl L-carnitine. Brain Res. 2002 Dec 13;957(2):223-30.

Permpoonputtana K, Govitrapong P. The anti-inflammatory effect of melatonin on methamphetamine-induced proinflammatory mediators in human neuroblastoma dopamine SH-SY5Y cell lines. Neurotox Res. 2013 Feb;23(2):189-99.

Miao Y, Ren J, Jiang L, Liu J, Jiang B, Zhang X. α-lipoic acid attenuates obesity-associated hippocampal neuroinflammation and increases the levels of brain-derived neurotrophic factor in ovariectomized rats fed a high-fat diet. Int J Mol Med. 2013 Nov; 32(5):1179-86.

Rosa FT, Zulet MÁ, Marchini JS, Martínez JA. Bioactive compounds with effects on inflammation markers in humans. Int J Food Sci Nutr. 2012 Sep; 63(6):749-65.

Maczurek A, Hager K, Kenklies M, Sharman M, Martins R, Engel J, Carlson DA, Münch G. Lipoic acid as an anti-inflammatory and neuroprotective treatment for Alzheimer's disease. Adv

Drug Deliv Rev. 2008 Oct-Nov; 60(13-14):1463-70.

Tarozzi A, Angeloni C, Malaguti M, Morroni F, Hrelia S, Hrelia P. Sulforaphane as a potential protective phytochemical against neurodegenerative diseases. Oxid Med Cell Longev. 2013; 2013:415078.

Sahin N, Akdemir F, Orhan C, Aslan A, Agca CA, Gencoglu H, Ulas M, Tuzcu M, Viyaja J, Komorowski JR, Sahin K. A novel nutritional supplement containing chromium picolinate, phosphatidylserine, docosahexaenoic acid, and boron activates the antioxidant pathway Nrf2/HO-1 and protects the brain against oxidative stress in high-fat-fed rats. Nutr Neurosci. 2012 Sep; 15(5):42-7.

Alfieri A, Srivastava S, Siow RC, Modo M, Fraser PA, Mann GE. Targeting the Nrf2-Keap1 antioxidant defence pathway for neurovascular protection in stroke. J Physiol. 2011 Sep 1; 589(Pt 17):4125-36.

Chen G, Fang Q, Zhang J, Zhou D, Wang Z. Role of the Nrf2-ARE pathway in early brain injury after experimental subarachnoid hemorrhage. J Neurosci Res. 2011 Apr; 89(4):515-23.

Medina AE. Vinpocetine as a potent antiinflammatory agent. Proc Natl Acad Sci U S A. 2010 Jun 1; 107(22):9921-2.

Jeon KI, Xu X, Aizawa T, Lim JH, Jono H, Kwon DS, Abe J, Berk BC, Li JD, Yan C. Vinpocetine inhibits NF-kappaB-dependent inflammation via an IKK-dependent but PDE-independent mechanism. Proc Natl Acad Sci U S A. 2010 May 25; 107(21):9795-800.

Herrera-Mundo N, Sitges M. Vinpocetine and α-tocopherol prevent the increase in DA and oxidative stress induced by 3-NPA in striatum isolated nerve endings. J Neurochem. 2013 Jan; 124(2):233-40.

Zhao YY, Yu JZ, Li QY, Ma CG, Lu CZ, Xiao BG. TSPO-specific ligand vinpocetine exerts a neuroprotective effect by suppressing microglial inflammation. Neuron Glia Biol. 2011 May; 7(2-4):187-97.

Han SG, Han SS, Toborek M, Hennig B. EGCG protects endothelial cells against PCB 126-induced inflammation through inhibition of AhR and induction of Nrf2-regulated genes. Toxicol Appl Pharmacol. 2012 Jun 1;261(2):181-8.

Tsai PY, Ka SM, Chang JM, Chen HC, Shui HA, Li CY, Hua KF, Chang WL, Huang JJ, Yang SS, Chen A. Epigallocatechin-3-gallate prevents lupus nephritis development in mice via enhancing the Nrf2 antioxidant pathway and inhibiting NLRP3 inflammasome activation. Free Radic Biol Med. 2011 Aug 1;51(3):744-54.

Sriram N, Kalayarasan S, Sudhandiran G. Epigallocatechin-3-gallate augments antioxidant activities and inhibits inflammation during bleomycin-induced experimental pulmonary fibrosis through Nrf2-Keap1 signaling. Pulm Pharmacol Ther. 2009 Jun;22(3):221-36.

Yang J, Han Y, Ye W, Liu F, Zhuang K, Wu G. Alpha tocopherol treatment reduces the expression of Nogo-A and NgR in rat brain after traumatic brain injury. J Surg Res. 2013 Jun 15;182(2):e69-77.

Flanary BE, Streit WJ. Alpha-tocopherol (vitamin E) induces rapid, nonsustained proliferation in cultured rat microglia. Glia. 2006 Apr 15;53(6):669-74.

Polidori MC, Mecocci P, Frei B. Plasma vitamin C levels are decreased and correlated with brain damage in patients with intracranial hemorrhage or head trauma. Stroke. 2001 Apr;32(4):898-902.

Golechha M, Bhatia J, Arya DS. Studies on effects of Emblica officinalis (Amla) on oxidative stress and cholinergic function in scopolamine induced amnesia in mice. J Environ Biol. 2012 Jan;33(1):95-100.

Golechha M, Bhatia J, Arya DS. Hydroalcoholic extract of Emblica officinalis Gaertn. affords protection against PTZ-induced seizures, oxidative stress and cognitive impairment in rats. Indian J Exp Biol. 2010 May;48(5):474-8.

Bhattacharya A, Ghosal S, Bhattacharya SK. Antioxidant activity of tannoid principles of Emblica officinalis (amla) in chronic stress induced changes in rat brain. Indian J Exp Biol. 2000 Sep;38(9):877-80.

THOUGHTS ABOUT YOUR BASE DIET

Over the years I've had the pleasure of helping a few thousand athletes fine-tune their diets and ergogenic nutrition plans. It all starts with a healthy base diet. You may be a young athlete just starting out in a sport, you may be approaching the end of your professional career, or you may be some place in between. Whatever level you are at, what you shove into your mouth makes a big difference to how well you perform.

You've likely heard top athletes say that diet is some percentage, usually a big %, of their success. How much nobody really knows. What I know is that a crappy diet will kill your explosiveness.

Young inexperienced athletes are the worst at maintaining a good performance diet. This is partly because they are on their own, or perhaps captive to their parents culinary expertise. College and professional athletes often eat at a training table which is managed by a team dietician. In other words, the elite guys and gals eat pretty well. But most athletes start out in pee-wee football, Little League, youth soccer, hockey, and the like, and then graduate on to high school sports. Their base diet generally needs a lot of help.

What's the big deal about diet? Explosive athletes (that's you if you're reading this book) rely on neuromuscular power- the nervous system making muscle perform with great precision, speed, and strength. Choke this process with a crappy diet and your performance suffers- guaranteed. So I ask you this- since you spend countless hours at practice, wouldn't it be a wise investment to make sure your nervous system and your muscles are so fine-tuned that gains in quickness, speed, striking force, and strength come often? A healthy nutrigenomic diet for an explosive neuromuscular system is your ticket to greater gains.

Working with athletes at many levels I find it's not only important to impart what nutrition is helpful to performance, but also what in the diet will sabotage performance. Let's get the performance landmines out of the way first.

Certain fats choke off both anabolic muscle growth and nervous system conduction. This means the nerves don't communicate with skeletal muscles very well and this reduces contraction velocity and explosive-endurance. Muscles burn bad fats dirty and spin off lots of free radicals which increase inflammation and this slows gains. You may not even be aware that what you are eating and drinking is sabotaging your potential because it sneaks up on you. If you learn to eat healthier you will experience a measurable increase in your athletic ability and your recovery speed over time.

Fast foods and packaged meals are some of the biggest roadblocks to performance because they're loaded with dysfunctional fats. Most fast food is built on quantity and not quality. I'm not against all fast food, just the food that is cooked beyond recognition and is loaded with grease, salt, and sugar. OK, that's a lot of the fast food sold.

I didn't include a bunch of meal ideas in this book because most authors that do so do it because they want to fill in the pages. I expect you to take charge of putting together healthy meals on your own because this is your responsibility. And if you're eating out I'd expect that you pay closer attention to what is healthy and beneficial to explosive performance, and what is really poor food you should avoid. So let's just boil down healthy eating to the following I've found is a good simple guide to eating for performance.

- Limit fast food to one meal a week. You can do this. Pull on your big-girl and big-boy pants and eat fresh often.
- Eat quality protein. Organic meats are best because they have a better fatty acid profile than factory farmed meats.
- Eat meat off the animal, not run through the micro-grinder. Avoid processed meats. For example, cook a chicken breast the night before and add slices to a sandwich.
- Don't eat anything fried. Fried foods are loaded with dysfunctional fats that are going to choke your muscles and nervous system. BBQ is likewise just not that healthy because cooked meats contain cancer causing compounds and also glycotoxins, although I must admit I BBQ fairly often- a weakness of mine that a performance athlete can ill afford to have. Do not eat French fries as they are loaded with nasty fats that clog cells.

- Eat veggies and/or fruits at every meal. Vegetables should be eaten raw or lightly cooked such as steamed. Organic is best because in general it is more loaded with phytonutrients like the polyphenols which can improve muscle sensitivity to insulin signals and nerve impulses for explosiveness.
- Don't drink much soda pop. They're loaded with mass produced ingredients like liquid sugar or high fructose corn syrup. Dark colored sodas like cola and root beer also contain glycotoxins produced in processing. Stick with water or tea to bathe your cells in fluid that's healthy.
- Consume tomato sauce and paste. They're loaded with lycopene, a carotenoid in the vitamin A family that has good intracellular protective benefits. Cook with a little olive oil as it helps with lycopene absorption.
- Cook with spices like rosemary, thyme, oregno, basil, turmeric, pepper, etc. These are great in small amounts at keeping cells sensitive, and inflammation in a healthy range.

Get creative and make meals from scratch. Eat fresh and up your plant based foods including fresh organic greens, fruits, seeds, and nuts. When possible, shop a natural foods grocery that carries fresh organic produce and organic bulk foods like rice, beans, seeds, nuts, and grains. Eat a variety of natural plant based foods along with lean healhy meats. Limit fast foods and prepackaged meals. That's my take on a base diet. Not a huge treatise, just common sense nutrition ideas.

Remember this: your body is your slave; it works for you.
~ Jack LaLanne

AVOID SPECIFIC SPORT NUTRITION INGREDIENTS OR PAY THE PRICE

There are ingredients in many sport supplements that should not be in them. The sport nutrition industry is a sub-category of the dietary supplement industry and old "health" habits are hard to break. For years, sport nutrition companies have been adding dis-adaptive nutrients to their formulas without even knowing that they can reduce performance.

Formulas designed by office confined nerds and guys in suits who haven't the slightest know-how of modern sport science, or what really goes on in the metabolism of an explosive trained athlete, are much to blame for creating the problem. Consumers fixated on antioxidants always being healthy should share the blame as well.

There is a failure to understand the role of "functional" stress in the adaptive response to training. Because of this, supplement companies get the ingredients wrong, the dose wrong, and the timing wrong. The result is that athletes improve at a slower rate with many never reaching their full potential. Fortunately, with today's modern science, this problem is avoidable.

New science research has exposed that many common nutrients found in hundreds of sport supplements are killers of reaction, power, strength, and muscle growth during adaptation from explosive training. Any nutrient that dumbs down your stress-response signaling molecules produced during training, like reactive oxygen (RONS), heat shock proteins, and myokines, runs the risk of bringing your hard work to a standstill.

The main dis-adaptive nutrients, when consumed above a minimum level for health, include excessive vitamins C and E, n-acetyl-cysteine, lipoic acid, coenzyme Q10, and likely some plant based substances with antioxidant activity.

What's excessive? I've been advising athletes to not consume large amounts of antioxidant vitamins for over 20 years. The supplement industry has waged a convincing campaign to push vitamins on non-athletes and athletes in just about every delivery system possible. Vitamins C and E in particular are found in flavored ready-made drinks (waters, protein drinks), pre-workout powders, post-workout recovery powders, nutrition bars, vitamin and mineral pills, cereals, etc. They seem harmless but they are not. Athletes should never consume beyond a near minimum of antioxidants so the stress response pathways can work their magic on the adaptive response from training.

In some cases additional vitamins C and E in the right form and dose can be healthy for seniors in poor health, but for athletes this is rarely the case. I never recommend antioxidants to explosive athletes because it's clear from many research studies (see some below) that they interfere with the adaptive response to training. I recommend you never consume a sport supplement with added antioxidants because these may reduce gains in muscle mass, strength, power, speed, and reaction. For this reason I rarely recommended multi-ingredient (e.g., 10 ingredients pre-workout and 25 ingredients post-workout) powder drinks, because they often contain dis-adaptive nutrients along with useful ingredients such as whey protein and creatine monohydrate.

I recommend only 60-100mgs of Vitamin C daily, preferably from foods and/or food based extracts (Amla, Camu Camu, Acerola, Kiwi, etc.) and 30 mgs (45iu's) for Vitamin E as a mixed (alpha, beta delta, and gamma) tocopherol in the "total" daily diet. It's likely that antioxidant minerals like selenium and zinc can blunt the adaptive response to stress as well. Your best option is to get your antioxidants from healthy foods like fruits, nuts, seeds, and vegetables and not get them from supplements, bars, drinks and fortified foods like cereals- unless you want to risk adapting poorly to training.

I know this new information cuts against the sport nutrition industry dogma and that operatives from many supplement companies will no doubt flail their arms and beat their chests and proclaim how wrong I am, but the extensive science doesn't lie. I'm just the messenger who's seen athletes perform better when they don't overload on antioxidant nutrients. It's easy to overload because the antioxidants are in just about everything these days. Check out the latest science below and decide for yourself.

Scheele C, Nielsen S, Pedersen BK. ROS and myokines promote muscle adaptation to exercise. Trends Endocrinol Metab. 2009 Apr;20(3):95-9.

Gomez-Cabrera MC, Ristow M, Viña J. Antioxidant supplements in exercise: worse than useless? Am J Physiol Endocrinol Metab. 2012 Feb 15;302(4):E476-7.

Powers SK, Talbert EE, Adhihetty PJ. Reactive oxygen and nitrogen species as intracellular signals in skeletal muscle. J Physiol. 2011 May 1;589(Pt 9):2129-38.

Ristow M, Zarse K, Oberbach A, Klöting N, Birringer M, Kiehntopf M, Stumvoll M, Kahn CR, Blüher M. Antioxidants prevent health-promoting effects of physical exercise in humans. Proc Natl Acad Sci U S A. 2009 May 26;106(21):8665-70.

Strobel NA, Peake JM, Matsumoto A, Marsh SA, Coombes JS, Wadley GD. Antioxidant supplementation reduces skeletal muscle mitochondrial biogenesis. Med Sci Sports Exerc. 2011 Jun;43(6):1017-24.

Kakigi R, Naito H, Ogura Y, Kobayashi H, Saga N, Ichinoseki-Sekine N, Yoshihara T, Katamoto S. Heat stress enhances mTOR signaling after resistance exercise in human skeletal muscle. J Physiol Sci. 2011 Mar;61(2):131-40.

Yamada P, Amorim F, Moseley P, Schneider S. Heat shock protein 72 response to exercise in humans. Sports Med. 2008;38(9):715-33.

Chung J, Nguyen AK, Henstridge DC, Holmes AG, Chan MH, Mesa JL, Lancaster GI, Southgate RJ, Bruce CR, Duffy SJ, Horvath I, Mestril R, Watt MJ, Hooper PL, Kingwell BA, Vigh L, Hevener A, Febbraio MA. HSP72 protects against obesity-induced insulin resistance. Proc Natl Acad Sci U S A. 2008 Feb 5;105(5):1739-44.

Poljsak B, Milisav I. The neglected significance of "antioxidative stress". Oxid Med Cell Longev. 2012;2012:480895.

Schoenfeld BJ. The use of nonsteroidal anti-inflammatory drugs for exercise-induced muscle damage: implications for skeletal muscle development. Sports Med. 2012 Dec 1;42(12):1017-28.

Barbieri E, Sestili P. Reactive oxygen species in skeletal muscle signaling. J Signal Transduct. 2012;2012:982794. Epub 2011 Dec 5.

Handayaningsih AE, Iguchi G, Fukuoka H, Nishizawa H, Takahashi M, Yamamoto M, Herningtyas EH, Okimura Y, Kaji H, Chihara K, Seino S, Takahashi Y. Reactive oxygen species play an essential role in IGF-I signaling and IGF-I-induced myocyte hypertrophy in C2C12 myocytes. Endocrinology. 2011 Mar;152(3):912-21.

Jackson MJ. Control of reactive oxygen species production in contracting skeletal muscle. Antioxid Redox Signal. 2011 Nov 1;15(9):2477-86.

Jackson MJ. Redox regulation of adaptive responses in skeletal muscle to contractile activity. Free Radic Biol Med. 2009 Nov 1;47(9):1267-75.

Petersen AC, McKenna MJ, Medved I, Murphy KT, Brown MJ, Della Gatta P, Cameron-Smith D. Infusion with the antioxidant N-acetylcysteine attenuates early adaptive responses to exercise in human skeletal muscle. Acta Physiol (Oxf). 2012 Mar;204(3):382-92.

Bailey DM, Williams C, Betts JA, Thompson D, Hurst TL. Oxidative stress, inflammation and recovery of muscle function after damaging exercise: effect of 6-week mixed antioxidant supplementation. Eur J Appl Physiol. 2011 Jun;111(6):925-36.

McGinley C, Shafat A, Donnelly AE. Does antioxidant vitamin supplementation protect against muscle damage? Sports Med. 2009;39(12):1011-32.

Gravier G, Steinberg JG, Lejeune PJ, Delliaux S, Guieu R, Jammes Y. Exercise-induced oxidative stress influences the motor control during maximal incremental cycling exercise in healthy humans. Respir Physiol Neurobiol. 2013 May 1;186(3):265-72.

Teixeira VH, Valente HF, Casal SI, Marques AF, Moreira PA. Antioxidants do not prevent postexercise peroxidation and may delay muscle recovery. Med Sci Sports Exerc. 2009 Sep;41(9):1752-60.

Zembron-Lacny A, Naczk M, Gajewski M, Ostapiuk-Karolczuk J, Dziewiecka H, Kasperska A, Szyszka K. Changes of muscle-derived cytokines in relation to thiol redox status and reactive oxygen and nitrogen species. Physiol Res. 2010;59(6):945-51.

Yfanti C, Fischer CP, Nielsen S, Akerström T, Nielsen AR, Veskoukis AS, Kouretas D, Lykkesfeldt J, Pilegaard H, Pedersen BK. Role of vitamin C and E supplementation on IL-6 in response to training. J Appl Physiol (1985). 2012 Mar;112(6):990-1000.

Michailidis Y, Karagounis LG, Terzis G, Jamurtas AZ, Spengos K, Tsoukas D, Chatzinikolaou A, Mandalidis D, Stefanetti RJ, Papassotiriou I, Athanasopoulos S, Hawley JA, Russell AP, Fatouros IG. Thiol-based antioxidant supplementation alters human skeletal muscle signaling and attenuates its inflammatory response and recovery after intense eccentric exercise. Am J Clin Nutr. 2013 Jul;98(1):233-45.

Ji LL. Modulation of skeletal muscle antioxidant defense by exercise: Role of redox signaling. Free Radic Biol Med. 2008 Jan 15;44(2):142-52.

AMPK Activating Nutrients and Explosive Training

In addition to being careful not to upset the adaptive response to stressors like RONS, heat shock proteins, and myokines by consuming antioxidant nutrients like vitamin C which is shown to blunt adaptation, you also need to make sure that AMPK and mTORC1 are balanced. mTORC1 is essential for mitochondrial growth, and therefore compliments AMPK. However, when AMPK increases, mTOR is decreased, and vice versa. So if you are training in a strength and power building cycle, where muscle protein synthesis is essential, you need to make sure that mTORC1 is far superior to AMPK. In contrast, if fat loss is your focus in a training cycle, you want to increase AMPK at the slight expense of mTORC1. It's a fine balance at times between mTORC1 and AMPK pathways and understanding them goes a long way to maximizing your specific performance goals. You want the whole package of lean explosive muscles.

Knowing that many nutrients can influence genes in the AMPK pathway it's important to make sure you aren't ingesting them in an mTORC1 skeletal muscle building cycle. Some nutrients shown to ramp up AMPK, and thus downgrade mTORC1, include chemicals in cinnamon, berry extracts, and spices. While these nutrients consumed in excess can be of great benefit to metabolically inflexible folks like the obese, diabetics, and the aged, they really have little use in performance nutrition focused on mTORC1.

SHOPPING FOR NUTRITIONAL ERGOGENICS

There are hundreds of sport supplements to choose from and manufacturers will spend thousands if not millions of promo dollars to joyfully proclaim that their supplements are the best. They'll cite some science, pay some athletes to endorse the supplements, and play to your naiveté.

They have a surprise coming. After reading this book you will never again fall for trickery, puffery, or scientific ignorance when it comes to selecting sport nutrition. You'll be armed with science based knowledge that will turn the tide and put you in command of your performance.

I've not only worked on the research and coaching side. I've also been active in the formulating and marketing of sport supplements as well, including training retail sales staff. I know all the tricks and I also know what's right for the athlete and their coach. I know that supplement makers would rather you simply buy into their pitch without question. You just can't. You can't because there is too much at stake. If you want to excel in athletics, compete with the best, be a starter, earn a scholarship, win a medal, or get big fat paychecks for years in the pros, you can't afford to be blindsided by pseudoscience and marketing fluff.

Is what I've presented in this book the perfect end all? No way. There's always room to improve and the science of performance for explosive athletes is growing at a fast pace. Each year there are breakthroughs that can help performance. There's much more science to come and more to question, learn, and apply. My job is to keep current so you can stay ahead of the curve- to arm you with truths and facts, not hyperbole.

As for buying ergogenic sport supplements, you already know they aren't cheap. Many are over-engineered which raises the price. Try to never pay full retail. If you shop at a store, look for the best supplements on sale. Order online whenever possible because the prices are almost always better, even compared to sale prices. Stick with proven nutrients and avoid the all-in-one many ingredient formulas. Avoid the artificial flavors, sweeteners, and preservatives that many bodybuilding supplements contain- they will do nothing for your training except perhaps screw with it.

"I think that from the time you start playing sports as a child you see that your responsibility to your team is to play the best that you can play as an individual... and yet, not take anything away from being part of a team."
~ Wayne Gretzky

If you're a coach, I wish you the very best with your athletes. You make a huge difference in their performance. Ponder, plan, and apply what I've presented in this book. Always look to ever-improve your nutritional ergogenic knowledge because the science is updating monthly.

If you're an athlete, I wish you many victories and championships, personally and as a team player, plus the great memories of your accomplishments and teamwork you will carry in your mind and your heart for your whole life.

Nothing in sports is achieved without paying the price of sweat, pain, and even defeat. Use the new discoveries presented in this book to design a better training plan. You'll be able to push harder and adapt more efficiently by using good ergogenic nutrients that will help maximize your gains in starting power, maximal speed, striking force, and power-endurance, as well as a reduced reaction time for faster starts. Always ask questions and use your common sense. Question everything and trust your good judgement. It's your training and adaptation after all.

With much love and admiration,
Rick

That which does not kill us makes us stronger.
~ Friedrich Nietzsche

PUTTING ALL THIS NEW INFORMATION TO PRACTICAL USE

As an athlete and coach I've viewed anything that has to do with sport nutrition with great scepticism. I've been to the sport supplement circus; I've seen the puppet show. The nutrition industry is rife with partial information, misleading information, and sometimes even fraud. Explosive athletes deserve better. That's why I wrote this book, to give you an edge, to empower you with a wide look at the science, so you can make greater gains in muscle mass, strength, power, quickness, and the like.

Ergogenic nutrition for explosive athletes is, in many ways, different than edurance or bodybuilding nutrition. It connects the muscle system with the nervous system to perform with great speed and force. I've listed some nutrient recommendations as a guideline to help you with your specific training plan. These are not set in stone and are basic ergogenic nutritional plans I've used and find them very effective.

Always remember that an ergogenic nutritional is a tool, not a miracle. It must be used within the right training plan to elicit the right response, be it focused on the mTORC1 pathway plus a neuromuscular component to build explosive traits, or the AMPK pathway to burn body fat. I know that what you've learned from reading this book is going to help you up your game. Now its time to plan your work and work your plan.

Rx

Name | **Young Athlete**

Training Cycle | **Strength and Power**

Supplements | **Whey Protein 20g for 1-2X daily**
Creatine Monohydrate 5grams/daily
Tri-Methyl Glycine 1,000-2,000mg daily
Mineral Orotates 1,000-2,000mg daily
Omega-3 Fish Oil 1,000mgs of EPA/DHA

This cycle is designed to increase muscle mass, maximal strength, and power traits. Training can be of high intensity and volume to maximize mTORC1 activity.

Name	**Experienced College Age and Beyond Athlete**
Training Cycle	**Strength and Power**
Supplements	**Whey Protein 20g for 2-3X daily**
	Creatine Monohydrate 5g daily
	Tri-Methyl Glycine 2,000-3,000 mgs daily
	Mineral Orotates 2,000-3,000mgs daily
	20-hydroxyecdysone 25-50mg daily
	Phosphatidic Acid 200mgs for 2-3X daily
	Omega-3 Fish Oil 2,000mgs of EPA/DHA

This cycle is designed to increase muscle mass, maximal strength, and power traits. Training can be of high intensity and volume to maximize mTORC1 activity.

Name	**Advanced College Age and Elite/Pro Athlete**
Training Cycle	**Comp Phase / Neuromuscular Explosiveness**
Supplements	**Whey Protein 20g for 2-3X daily**
	Creatine Monohydrate 5g daily
	Tri-Methyl Glycine 1,000-2,000 mgs daily
	Mineral Orotates 1,000-2,000mgs daily
	Mineral Succinates 1,000mgs
	Omega-3 Fish Oil 2,000mgs of EPA/DHA
Day of Competition	**α-GPC 400mg 3x/day (1,200mgs total)**
	Huperzine A 100-200mcgs 30 min before
	Vitamin B6 as P5P 30mgs, and B12 as methylcobalamin 1,000-2,000mcg's
	Caffeine 400mg-800mg (low-high body weight dependent) before comp.

Name	**Fat Burning AMPK Cycle**
Training Cycle	**Off season fat burning prep strength**
Supplements	**Whey Protein 20g for 1-2X daily** **AMPK cocktail with green coffee bean extract (200mgs cholorgenic acid), trans-Resveratrol 20mg, Green Tea extract (150mg EGCG), Black Pepper extract (as Bioperine® 5mg) for 2x daily with dose 30min prior to HIIT exercise.**

HIIT in AM after all night fast. Do not eat for 1 hour after HIIT workout. If you do a HIIT PM workout, again fast 1 hr prior to and 1 hr after HIIT. Limit carbs during the day to ultra-low glycemic and consume carbs 1hr after PM workout. Limit fats to lean meats and fish, some olive oil or flax oil with apple cider vinegar (rich in acetic acid).

Rx

Name — **Concussion Prevention & Post Game**

Training Cycle — **In Season**

Supplements — **Omega-3 Fish Oil 2,000mgs of EPA/DHA**
Creatine Monohydrate 5 grams
Acetyl-L-Carnitine 500mgs for 2x/day
Vinpocetine 10mgs 1-2x daily.
Lipoic Acid 100-200 mgs twice daily
Green Tea 400mgs (50% EGCG) daily

Begin taking supplement cocktail 1 day prior and day of competition, and 1-2 days after competition. If you experience brain trauma notify your health care team immediately.

Made in the USA
Charleston, SC
14 June 2016